Origami for Kids

Young Scholar

Young Scholar
An imprint of Ciparum LLC

Origami for Kids
© 2017 Ciparum LLC
All rights reserved.
ISBN-10:1-63589-509-X
ISBN-13:978-1-63589-509-4

www.youngscholar.co

Origami for Kids

Table of Contents

Bear

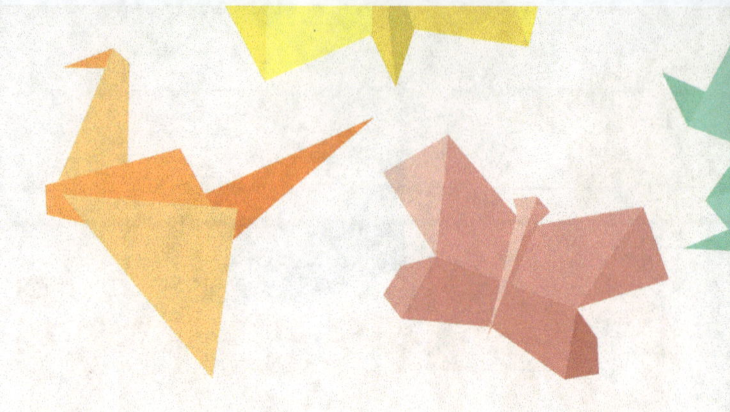

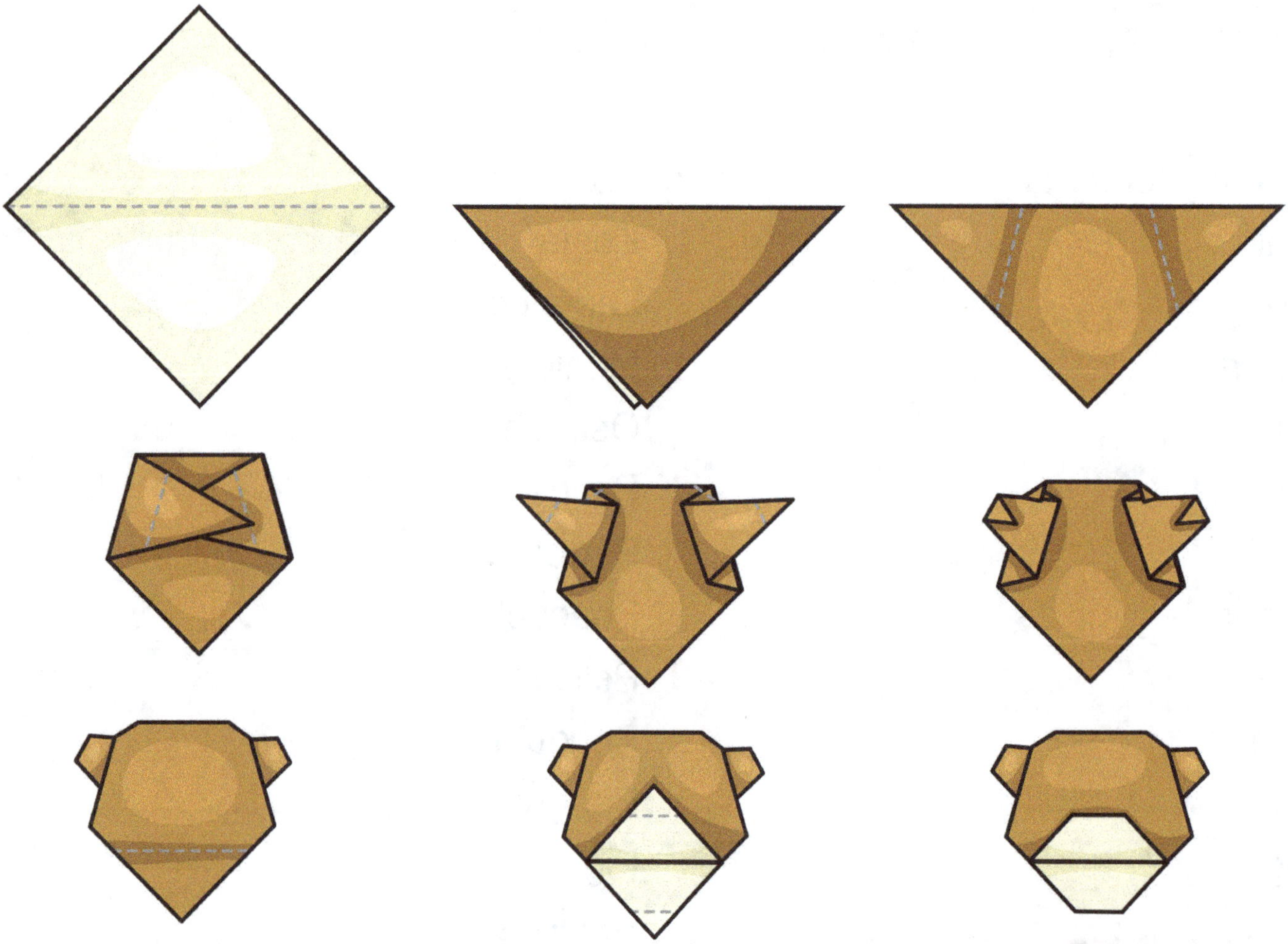

Bear

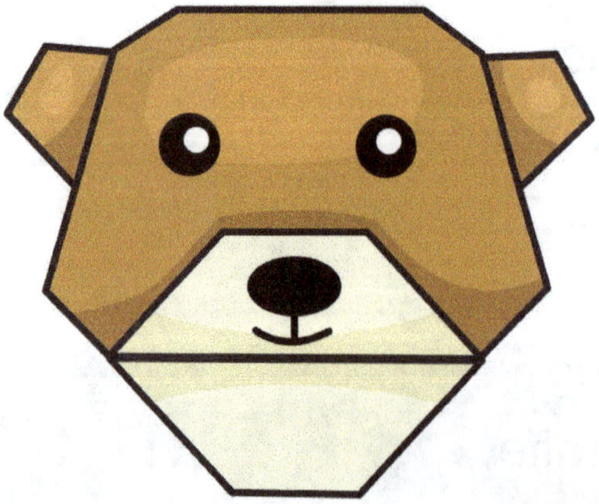

Cat

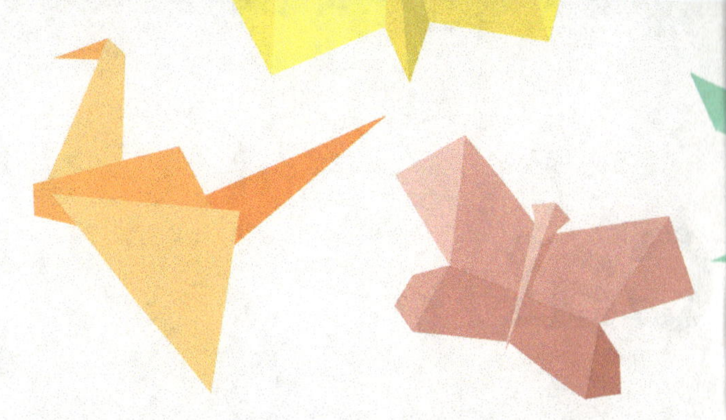

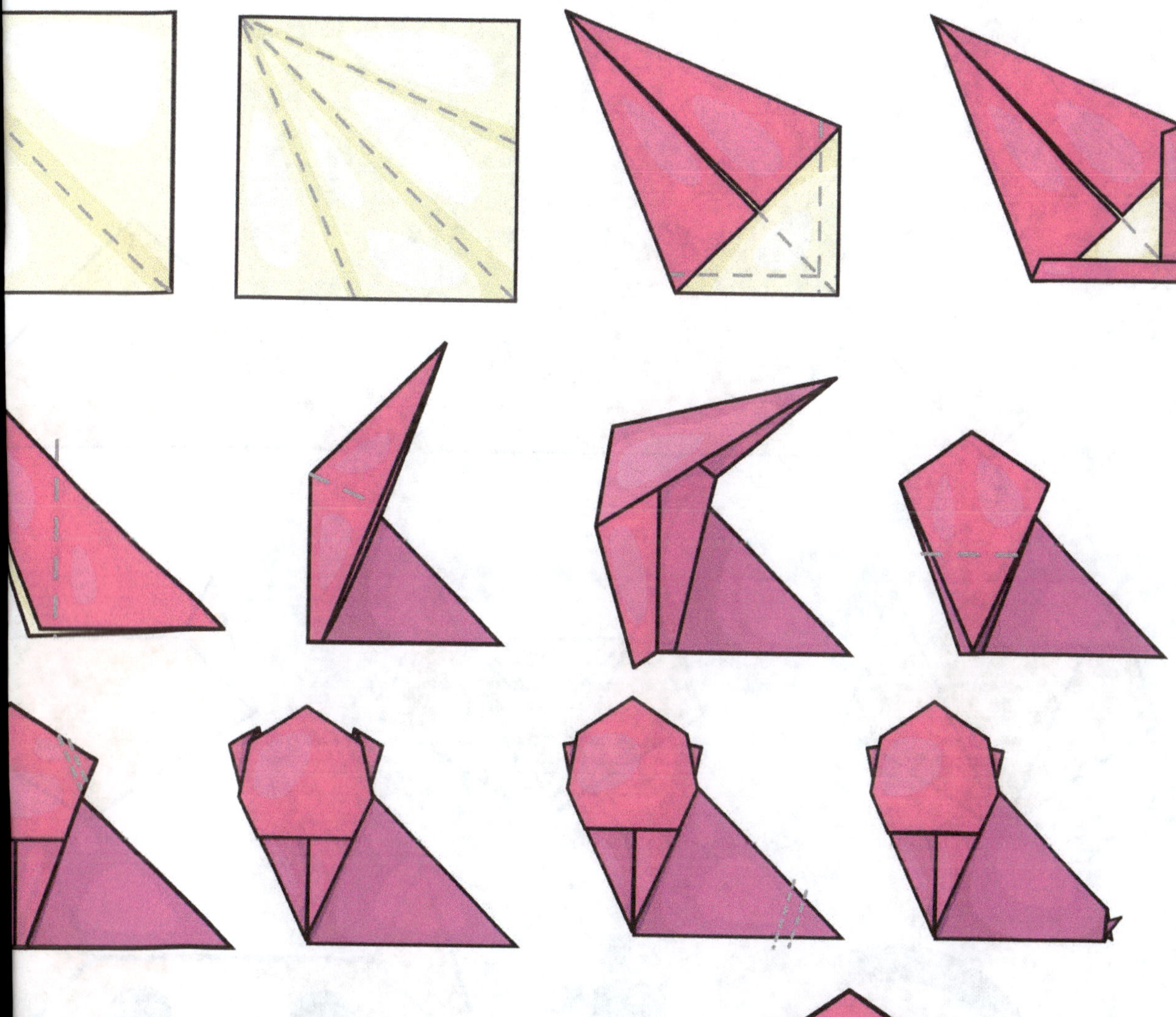

Cat

Bee

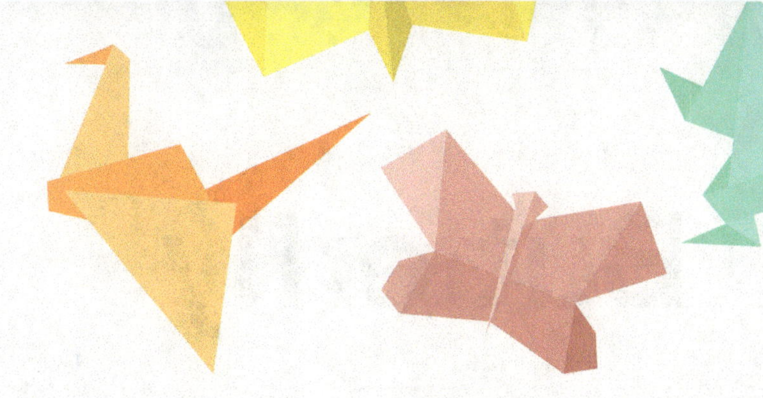

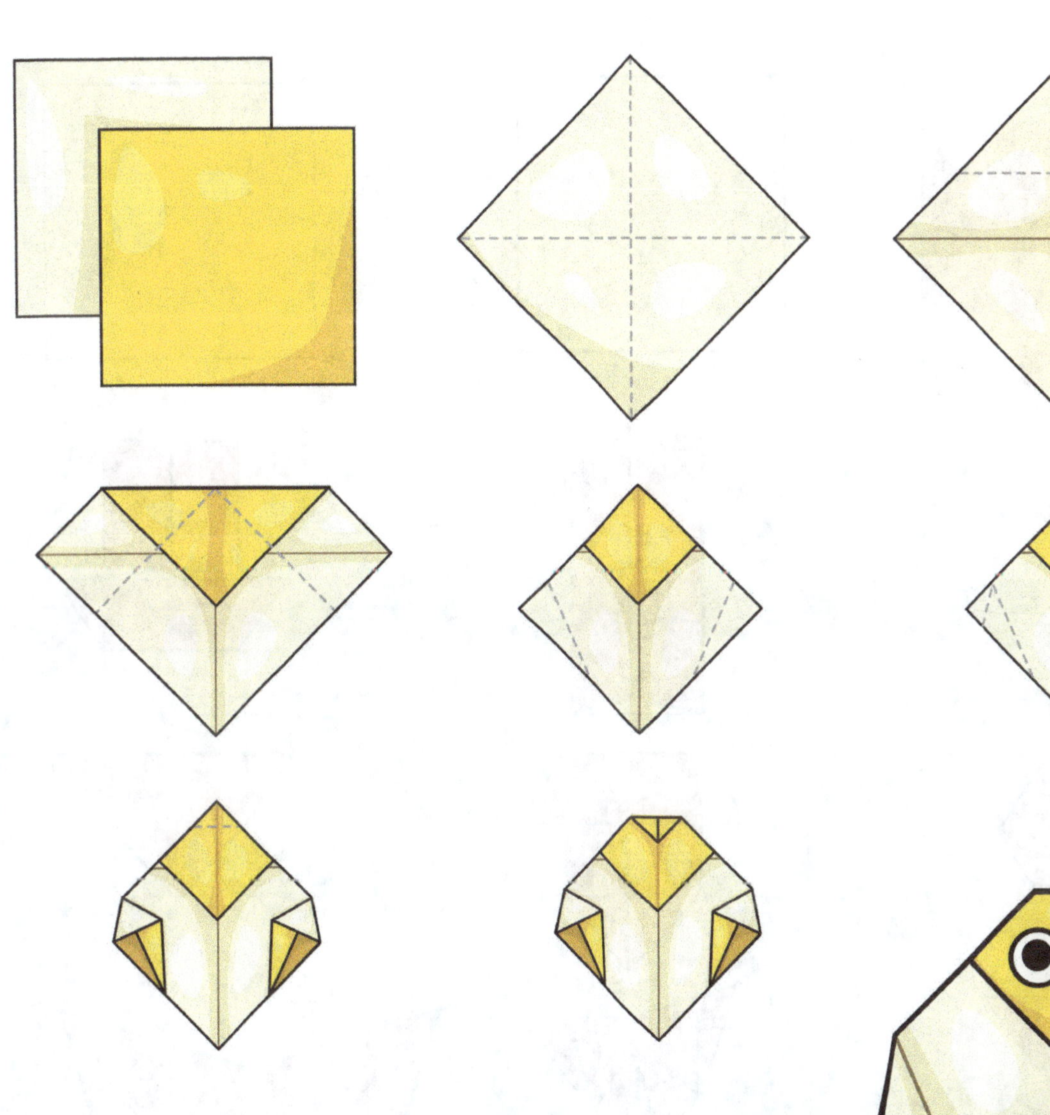

Bee

Butterfly

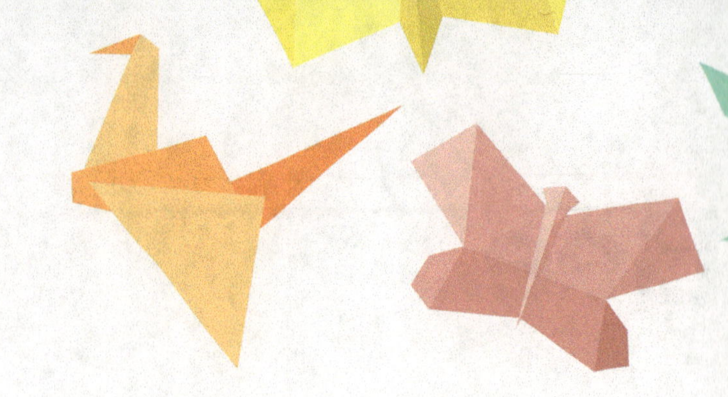

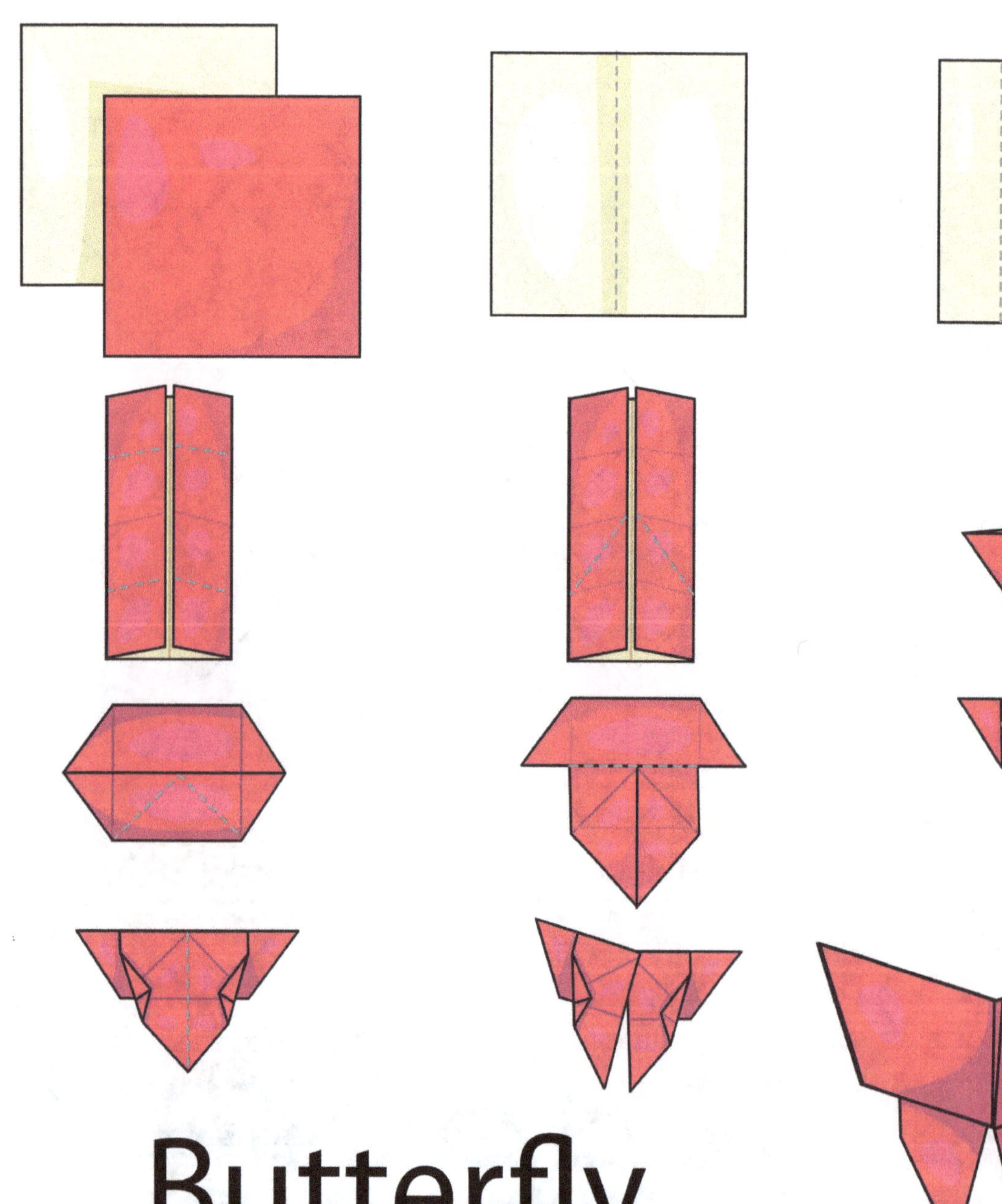

Butterfly

Cat

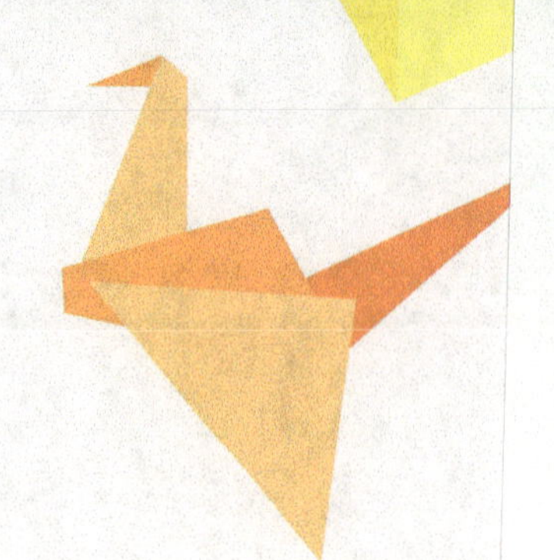

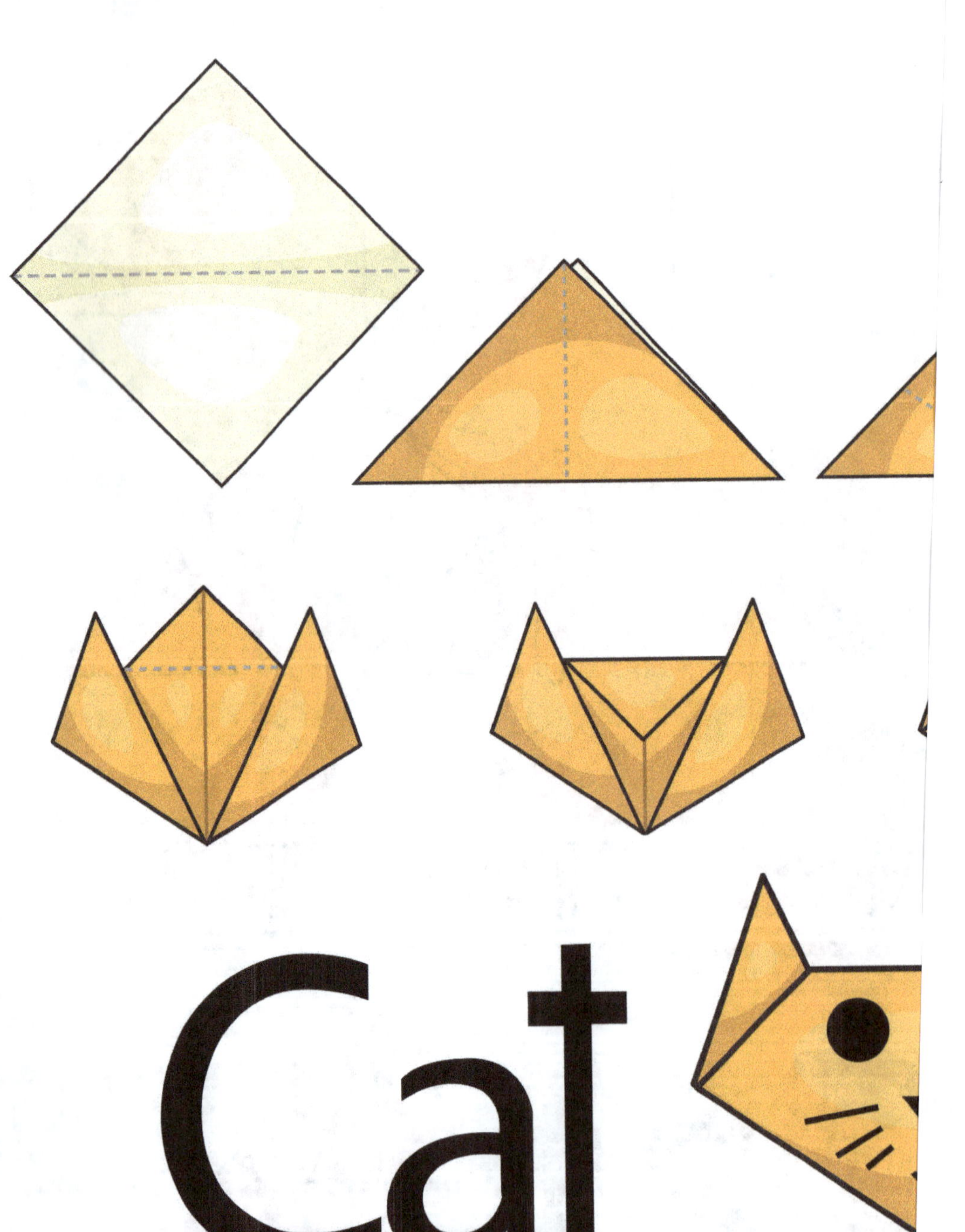

Bee

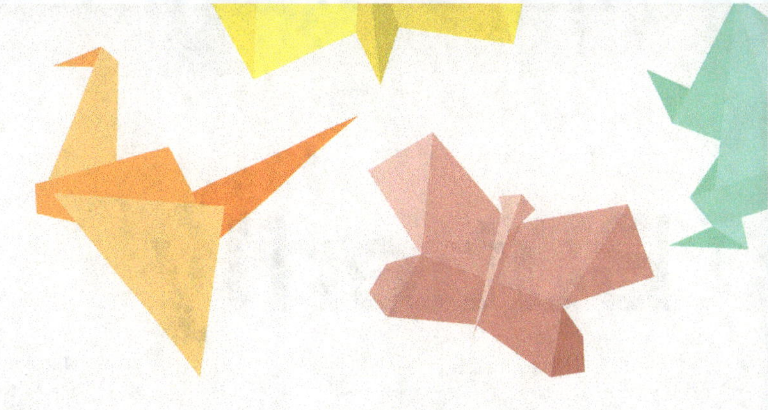

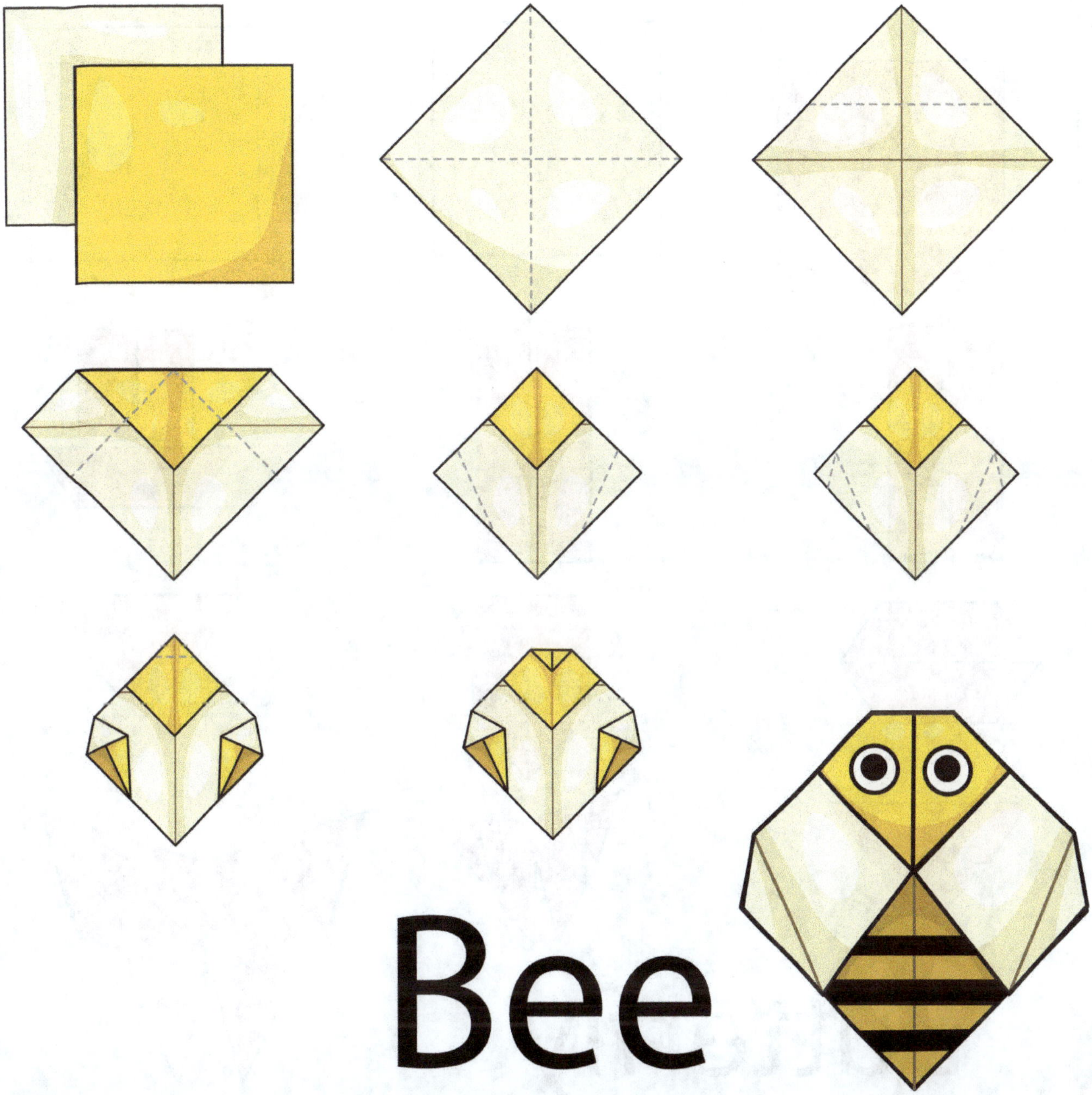

Bee

Butterfly

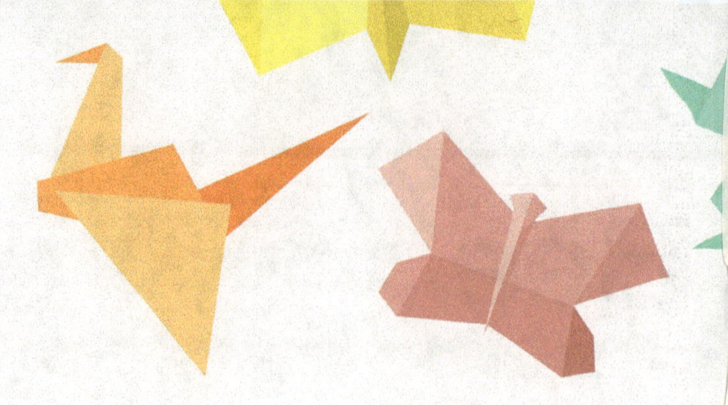

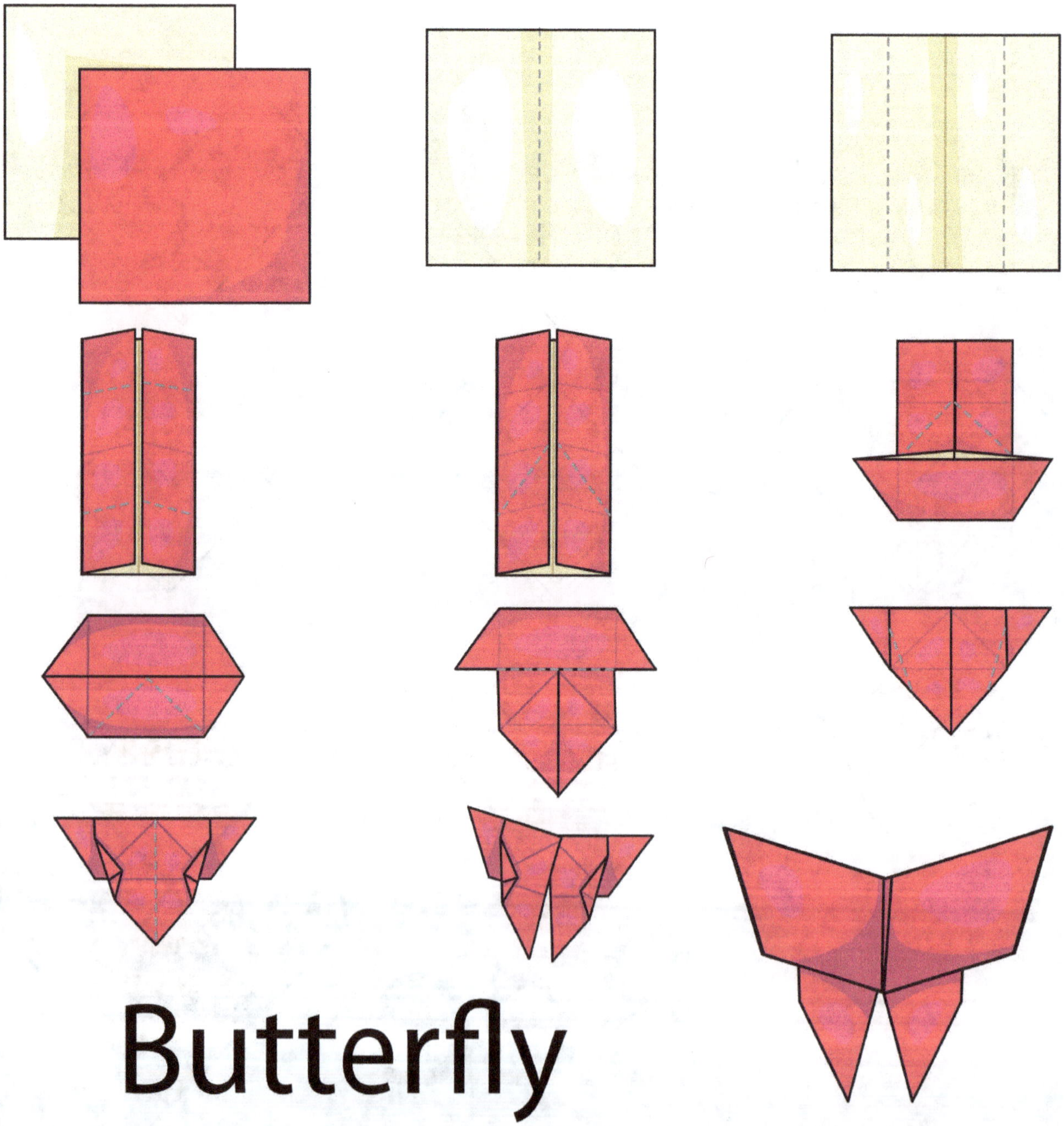

Butterfly

Cat

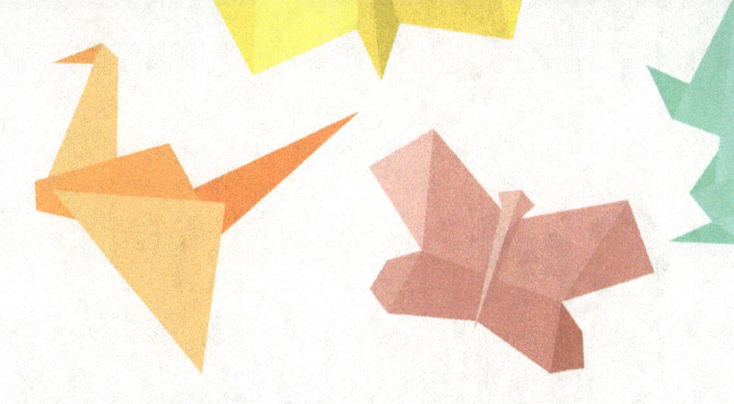

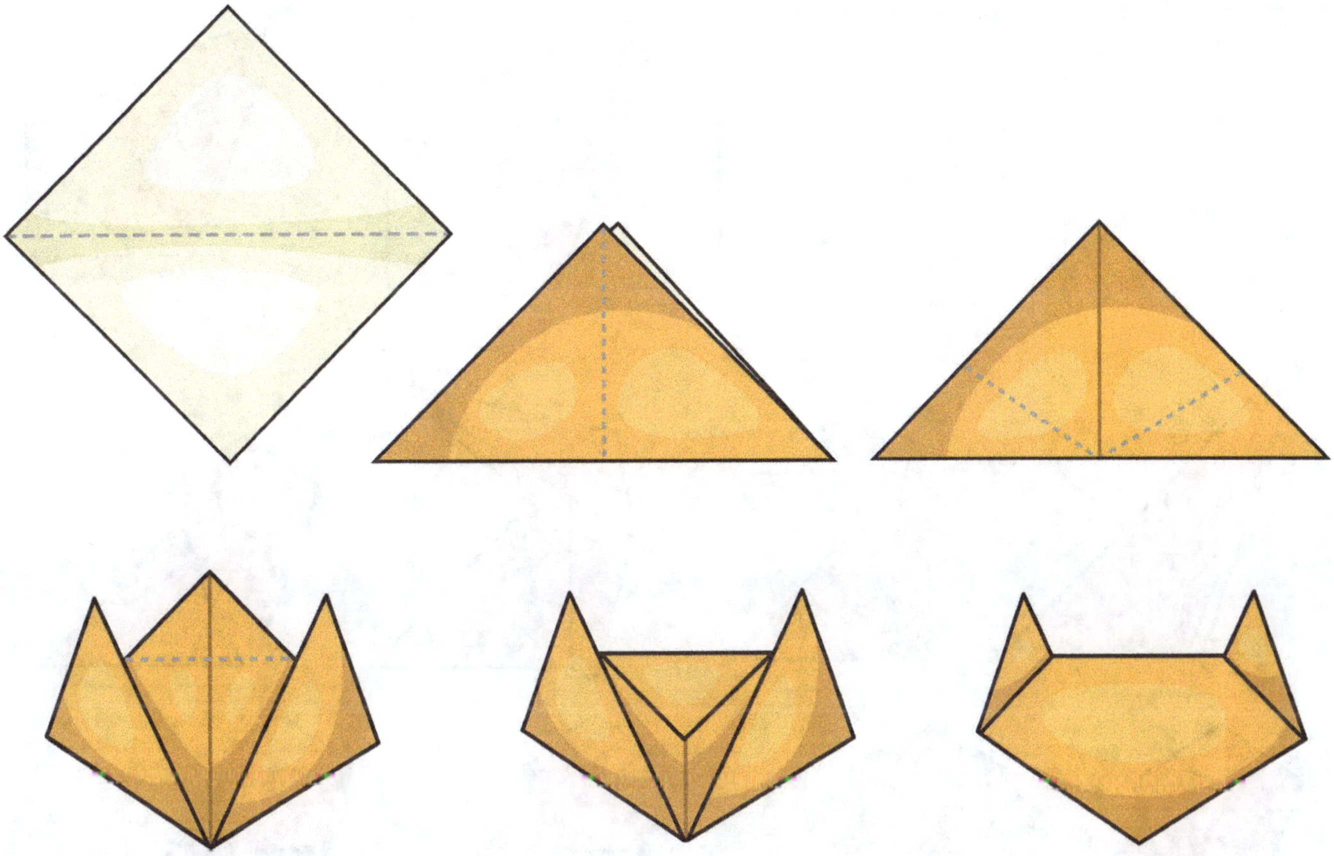

Cat

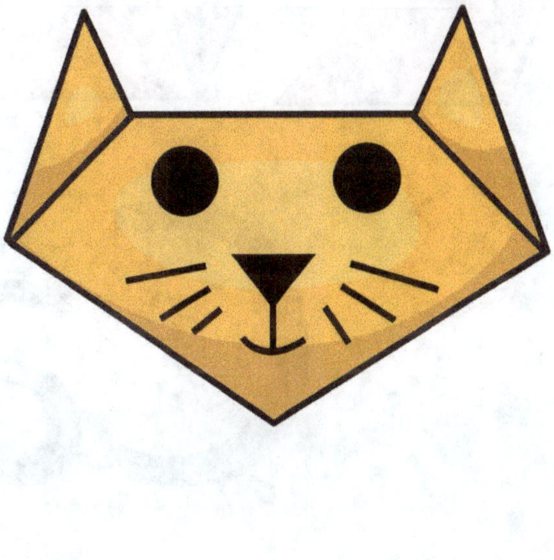

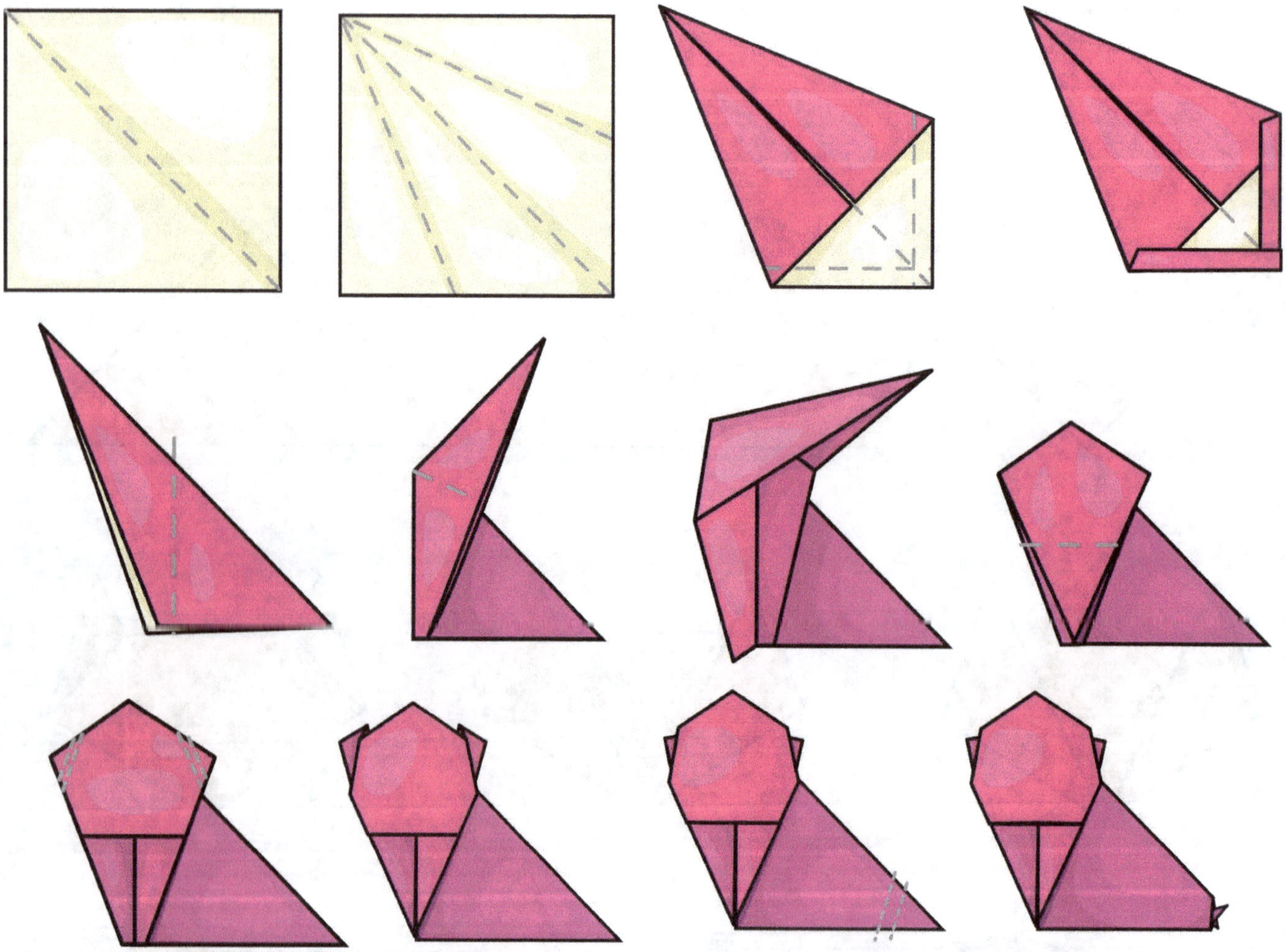

Cat

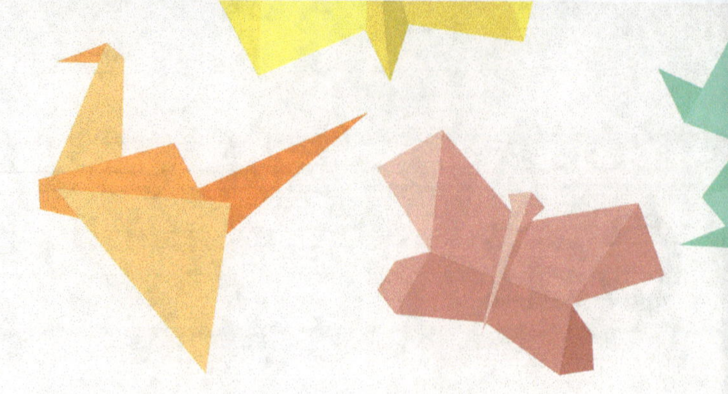

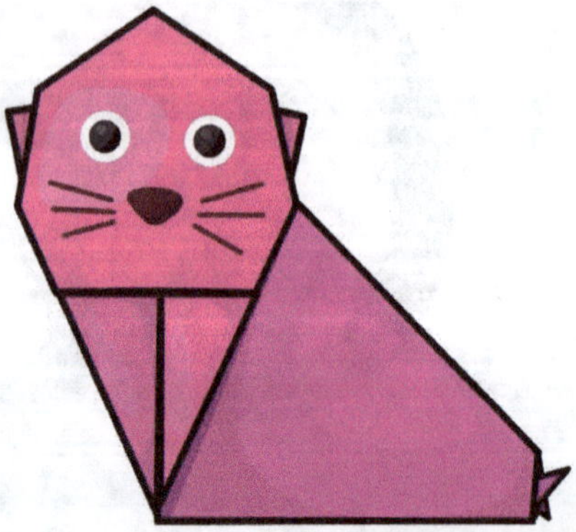

Chick

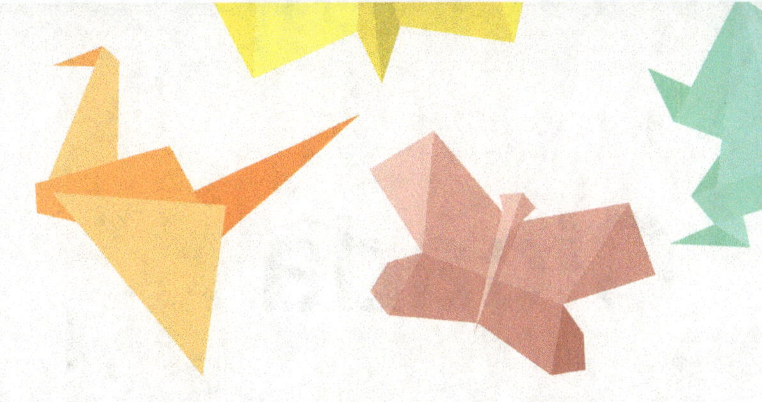

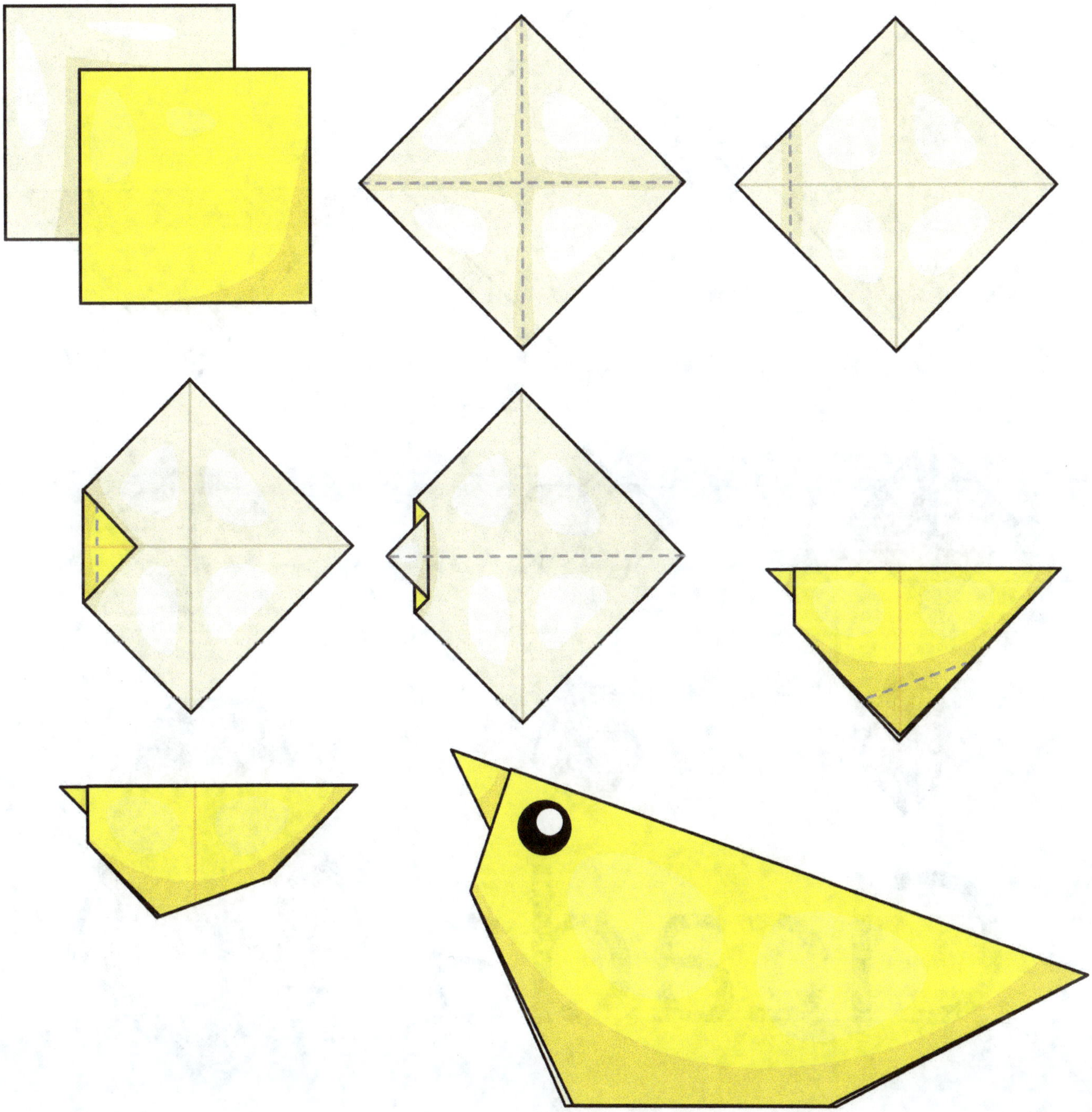

Cicada

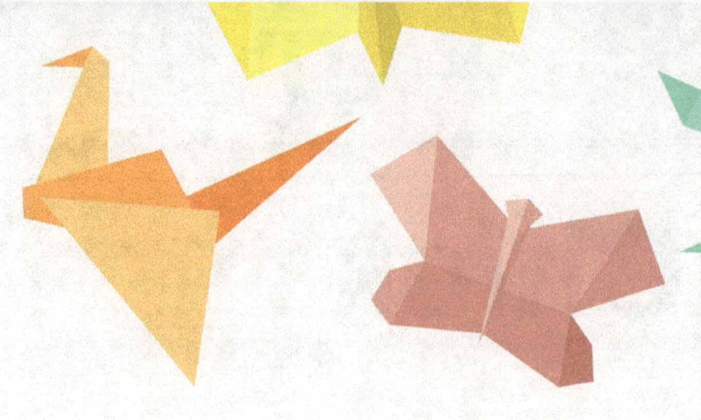

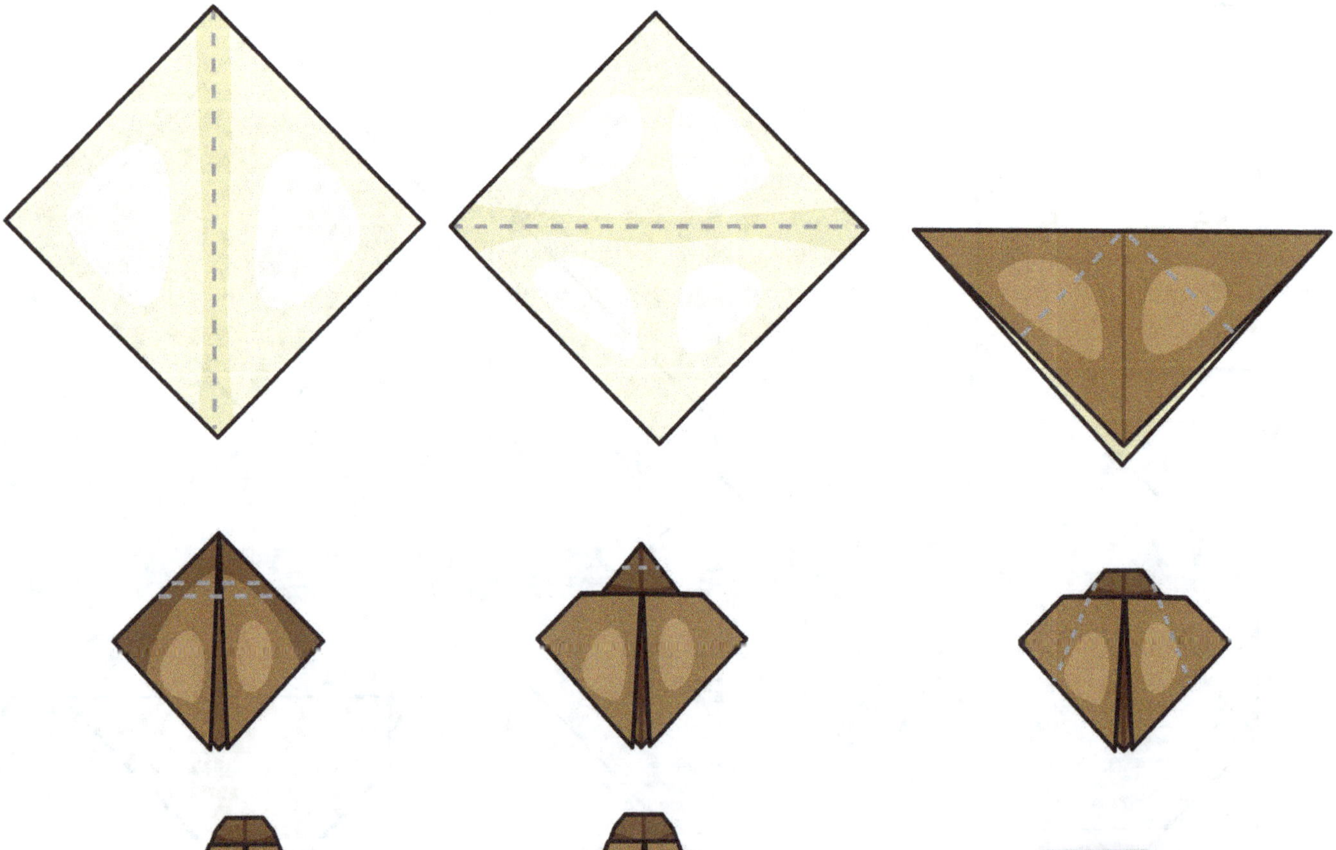

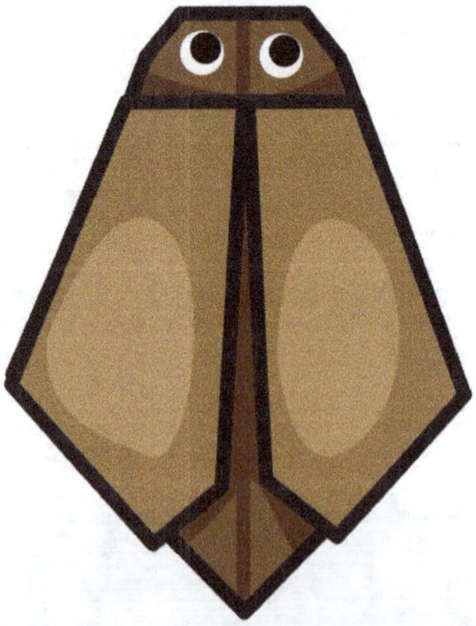

Cicada

Cow

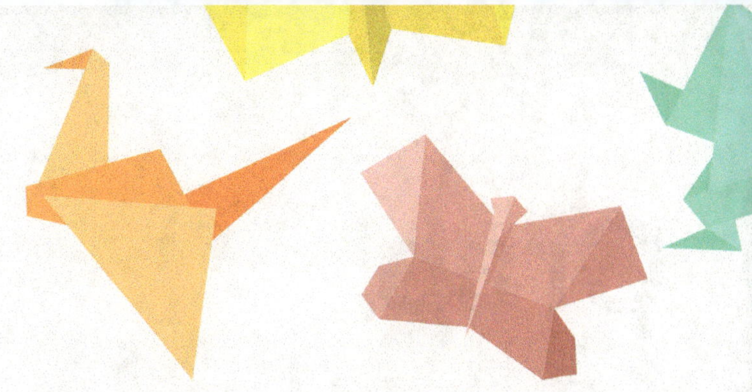

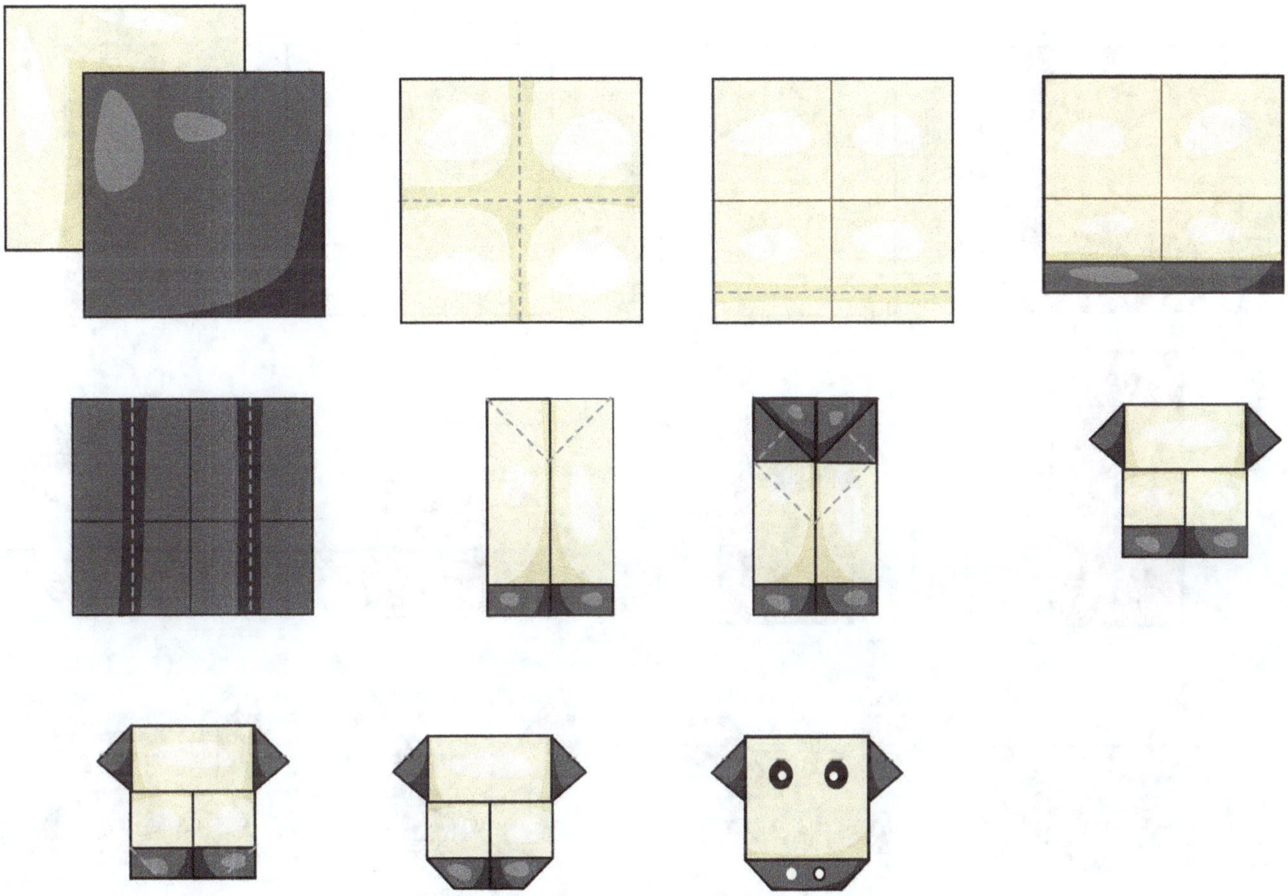

Cow

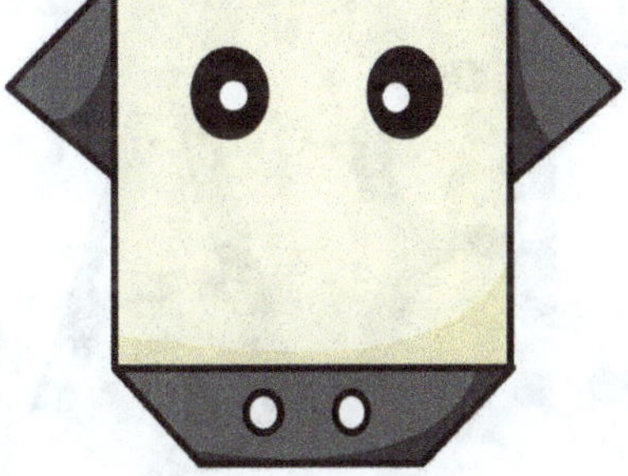

Crab

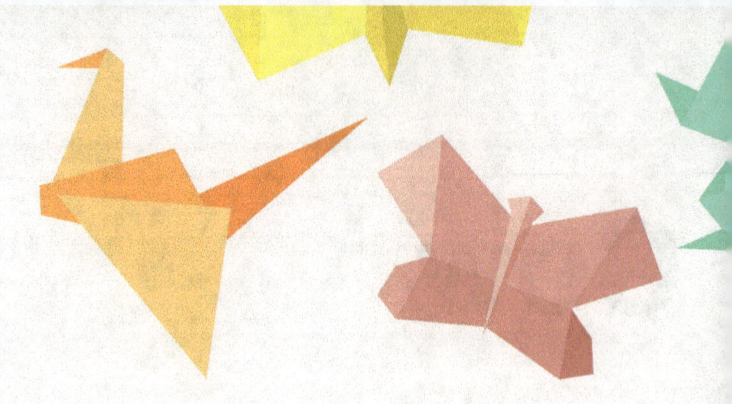

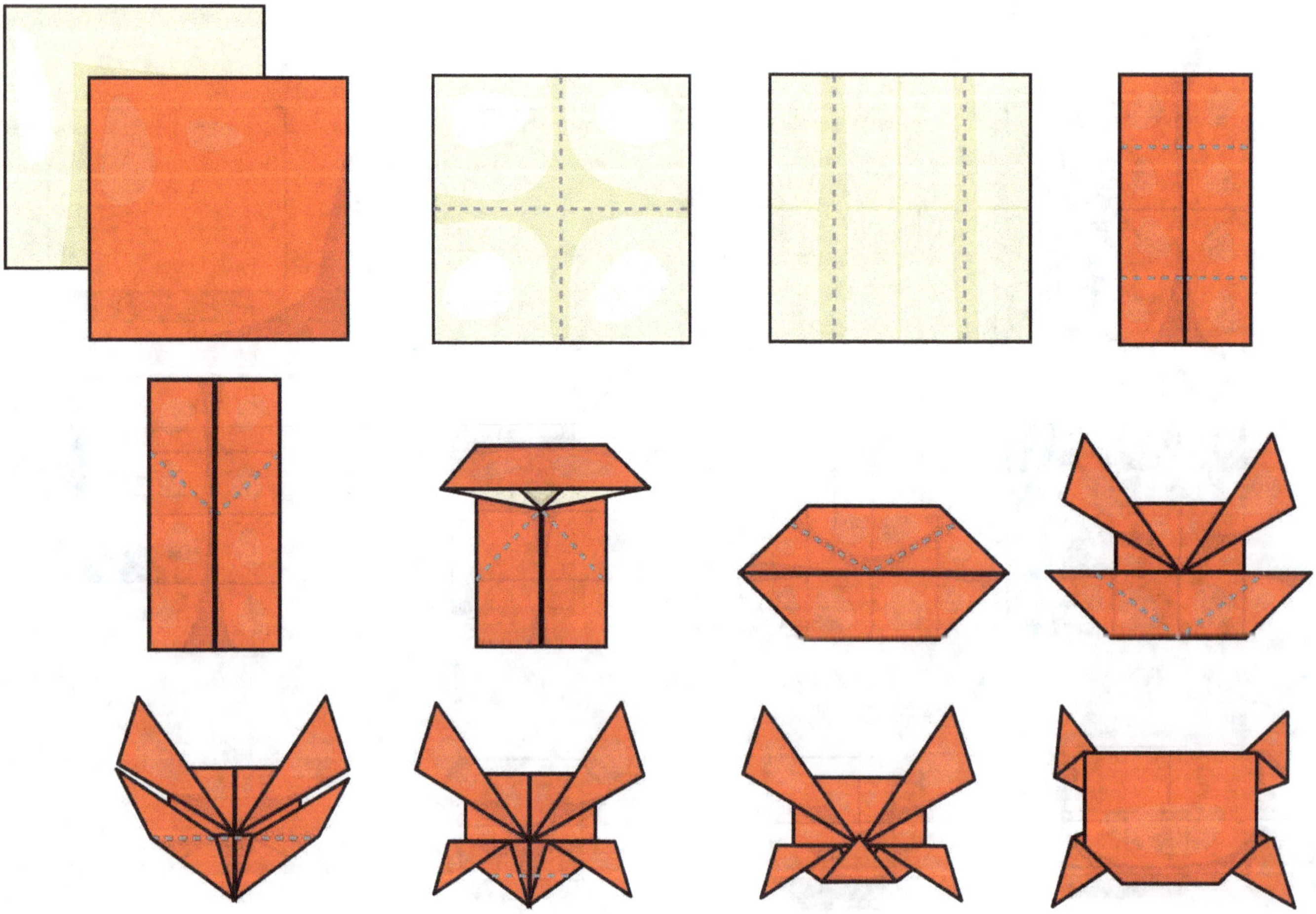

CRAB

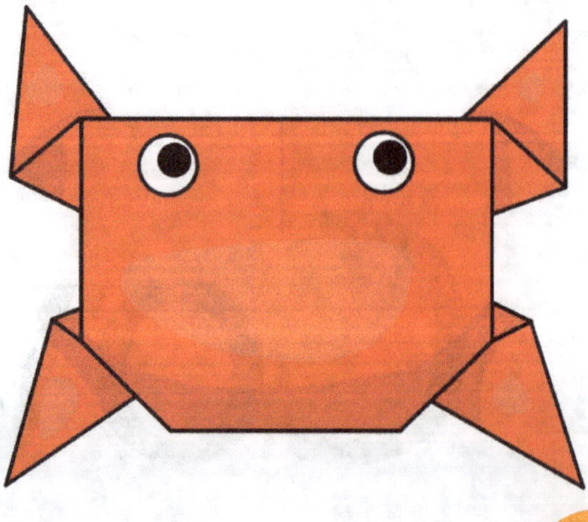

Crow

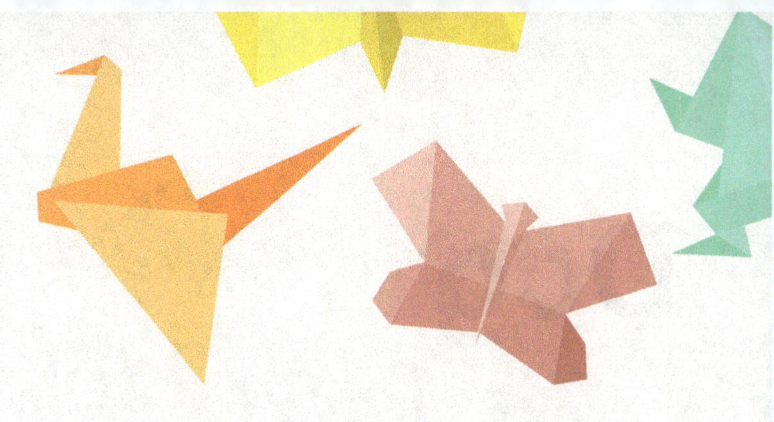

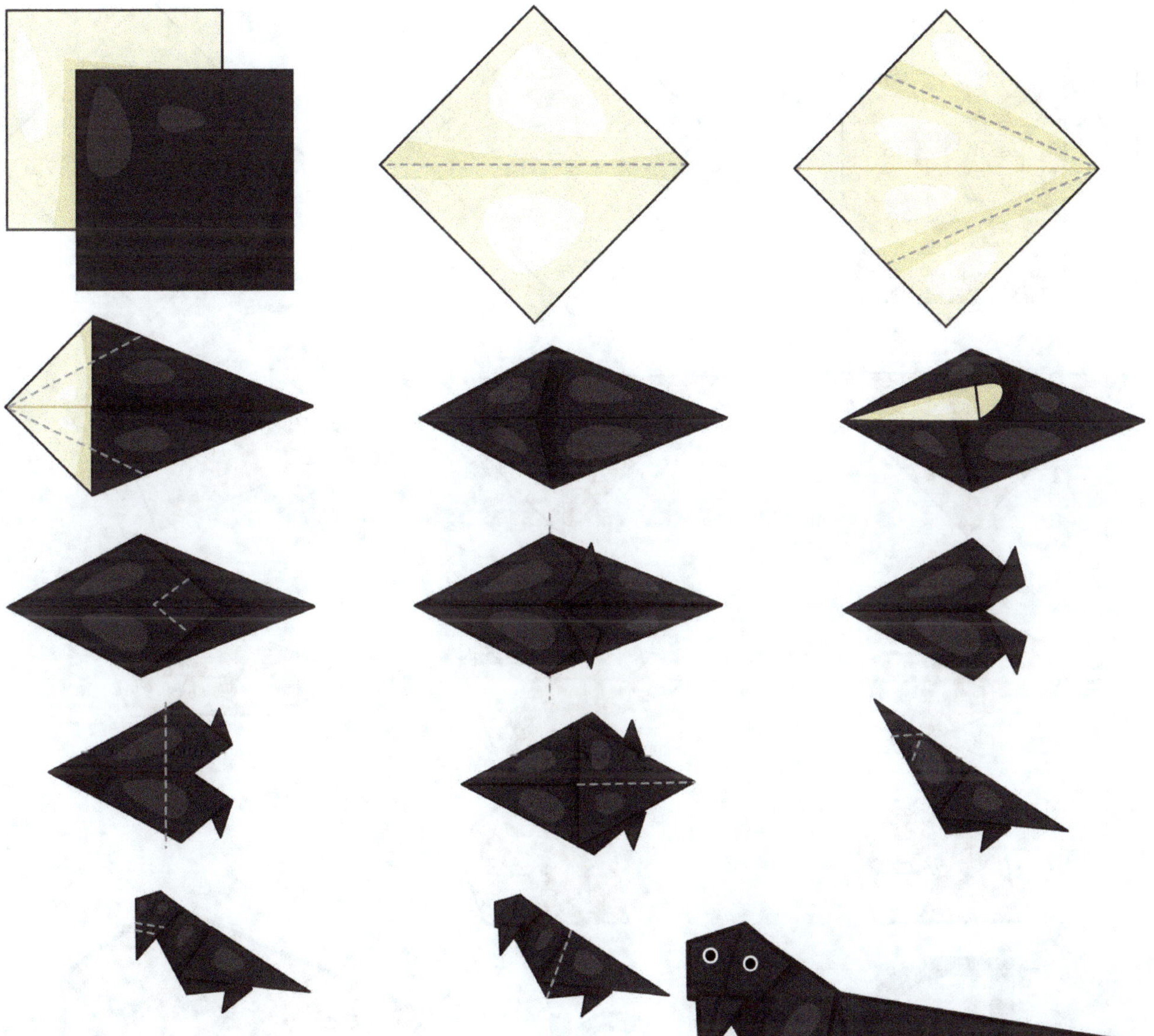

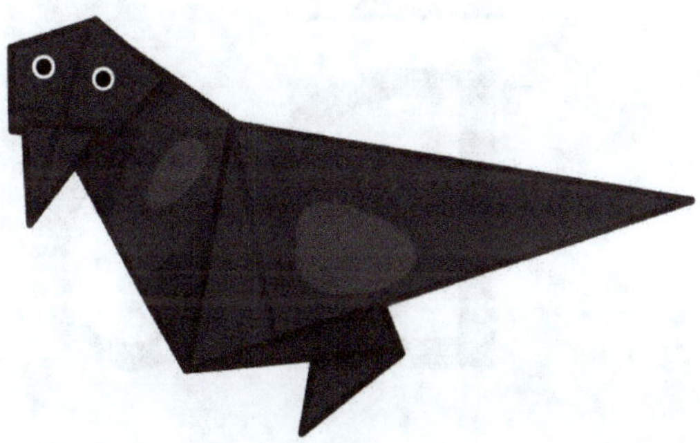

Crow

Dog

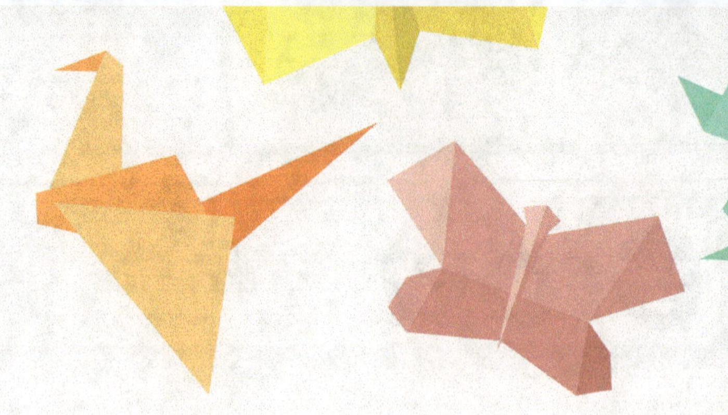

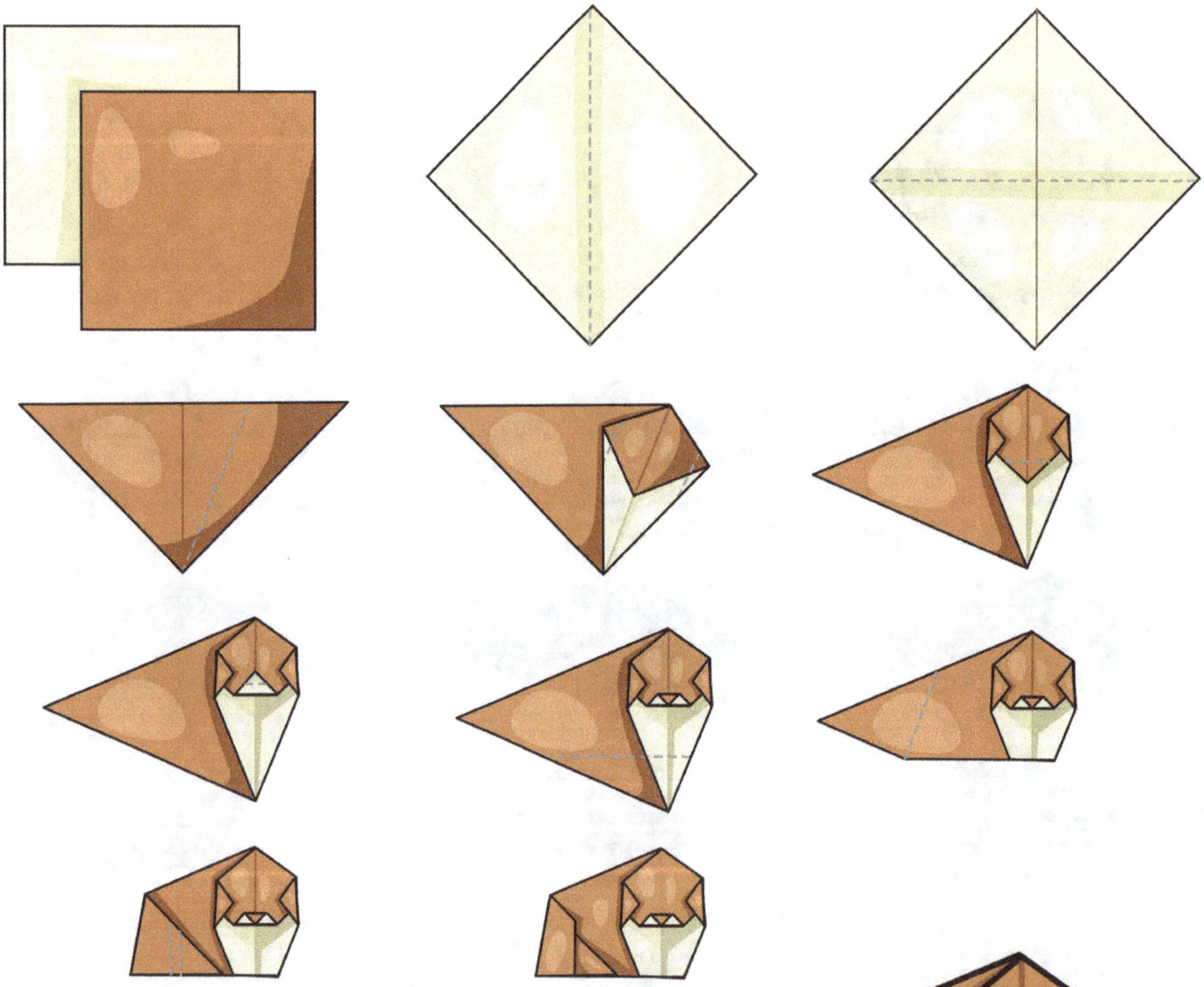

Dog

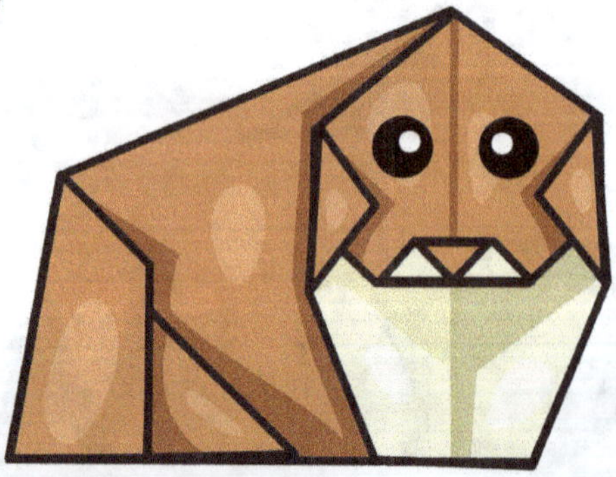

Duck

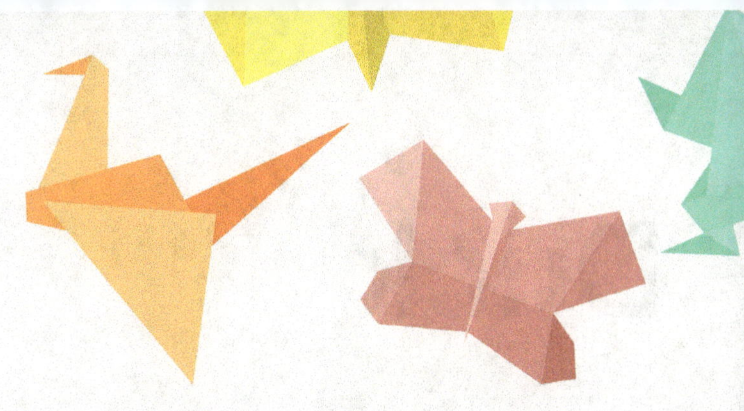

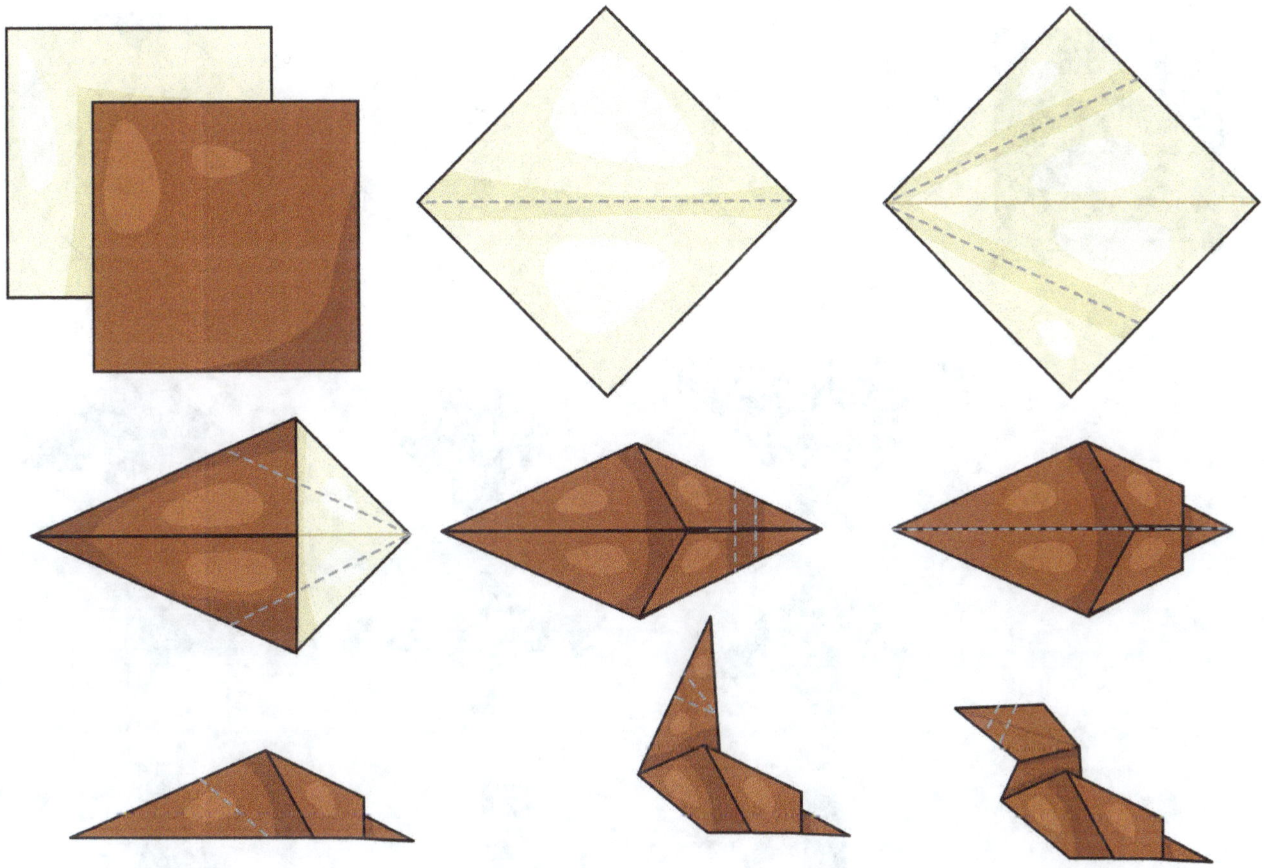

Wild Duck

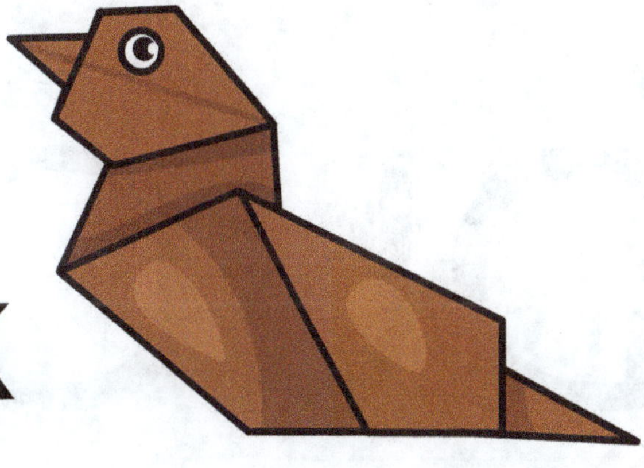

Duck

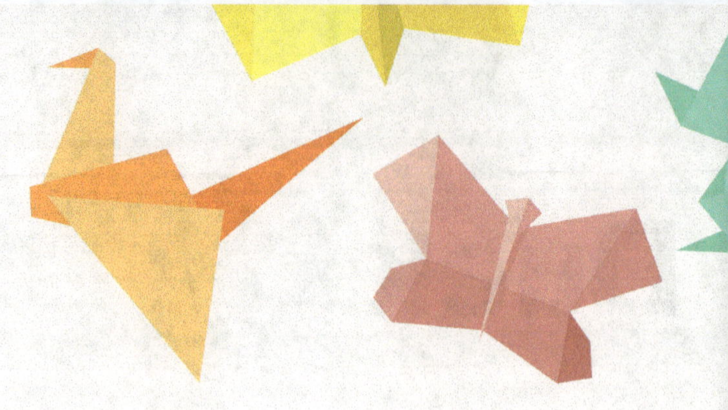

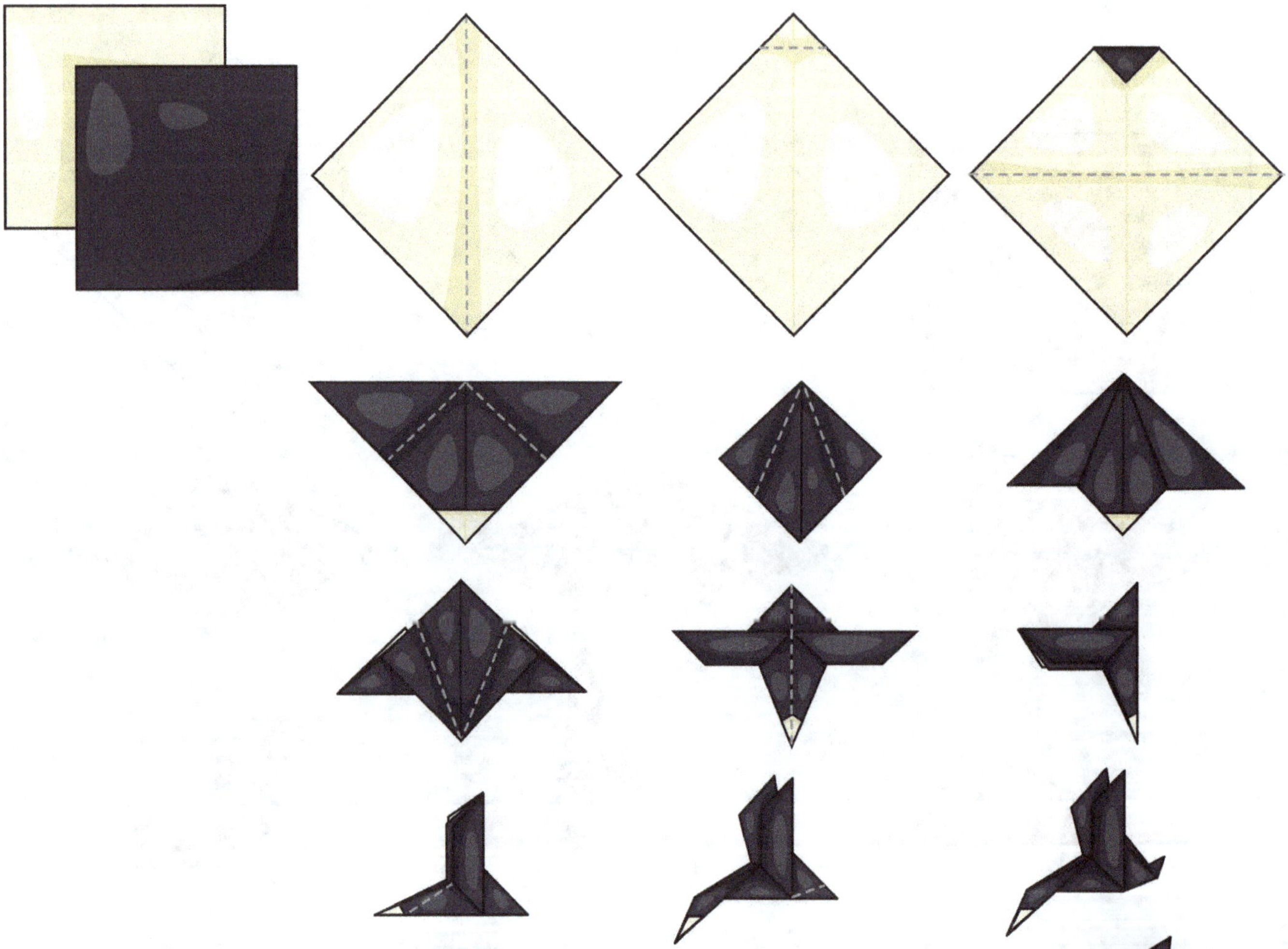

DUCK

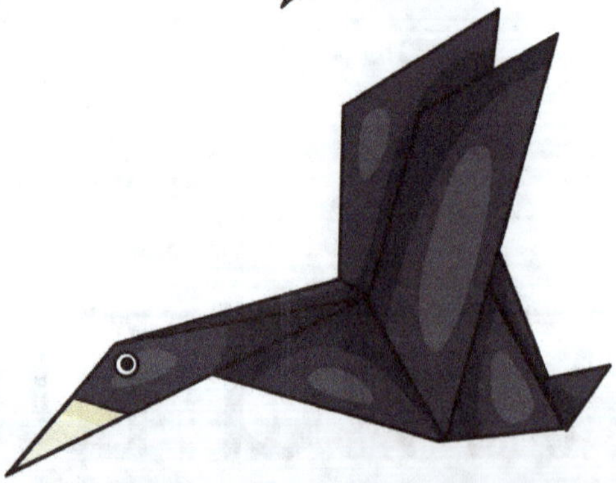

Elephant

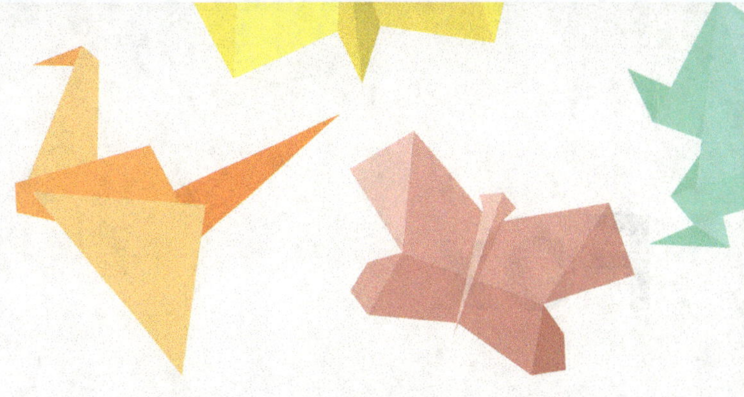

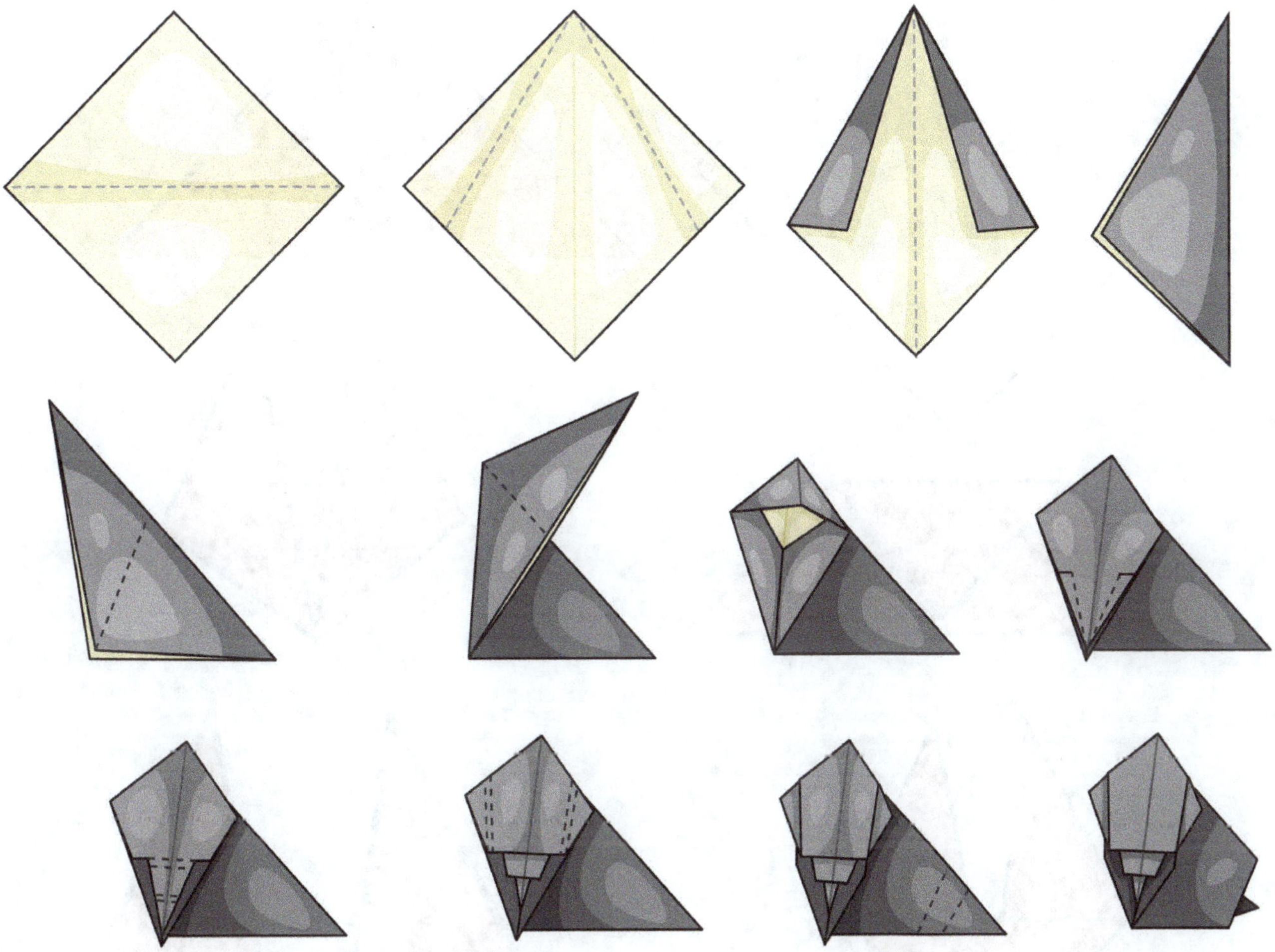

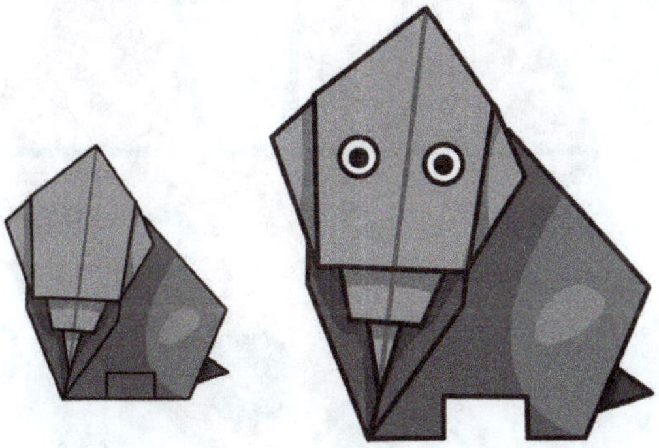

Elephant

Fox

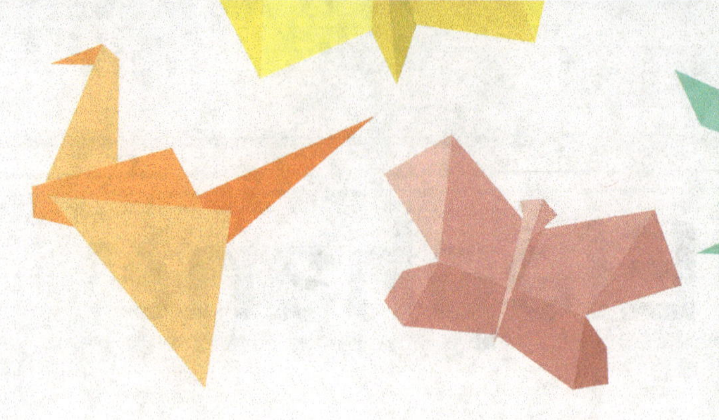

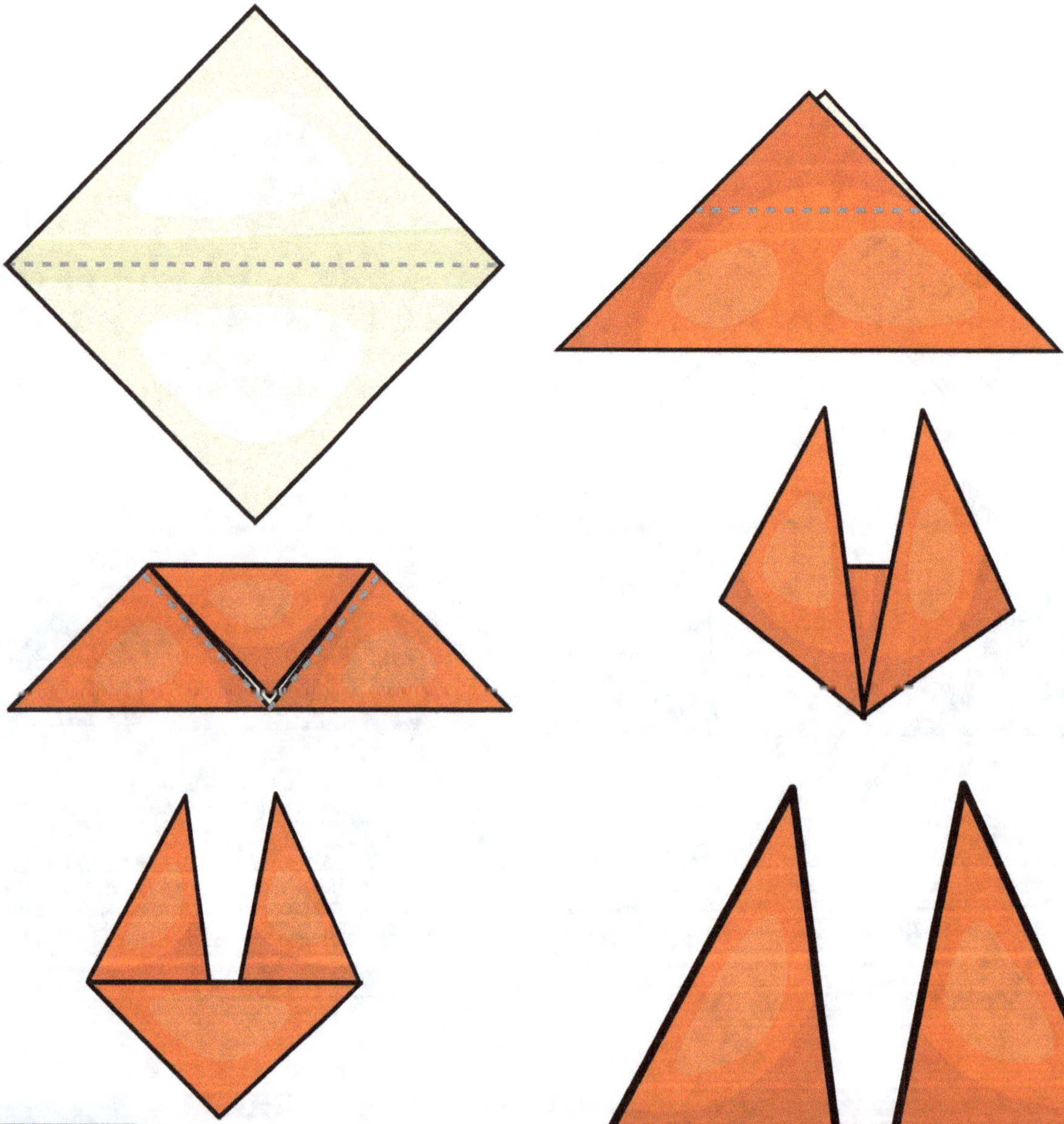

Fox

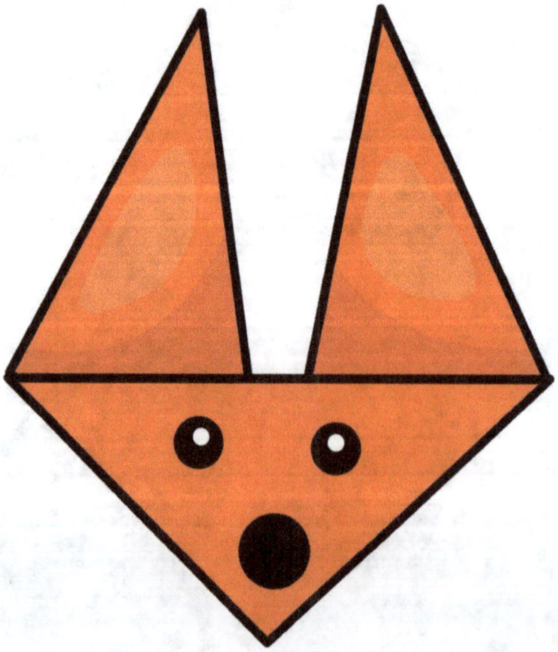

Fox

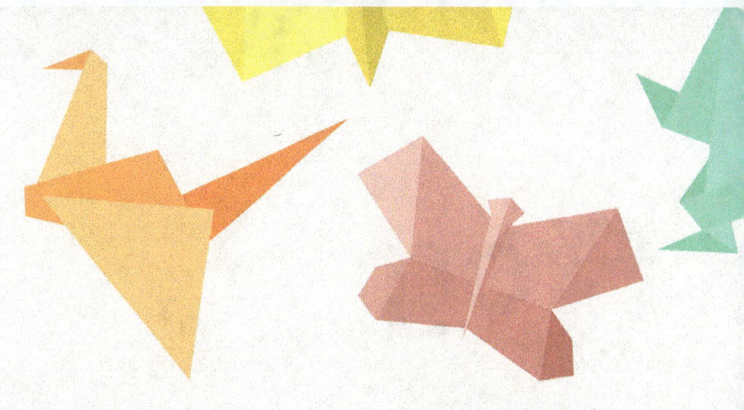

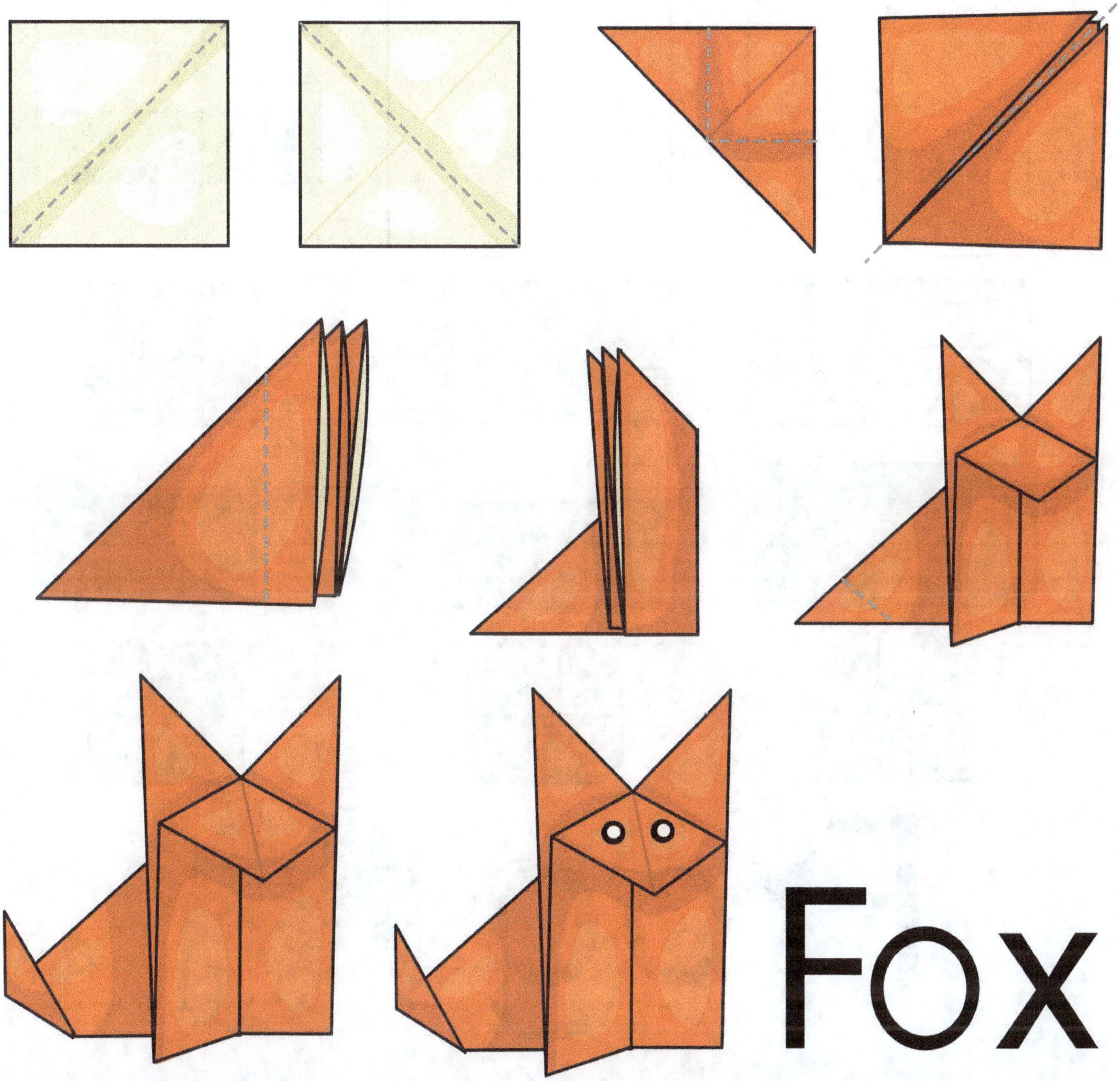

Fox

Frog

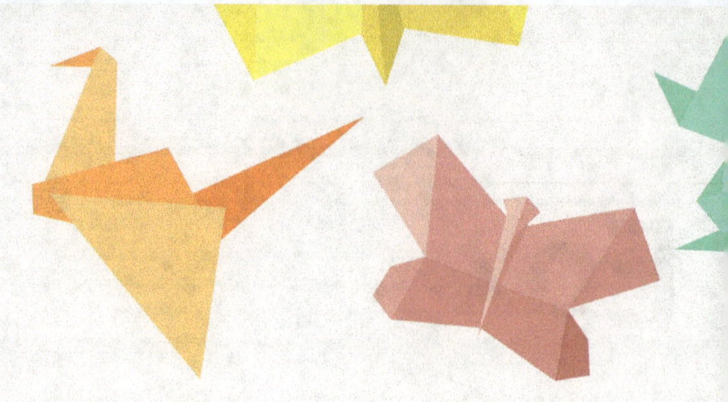

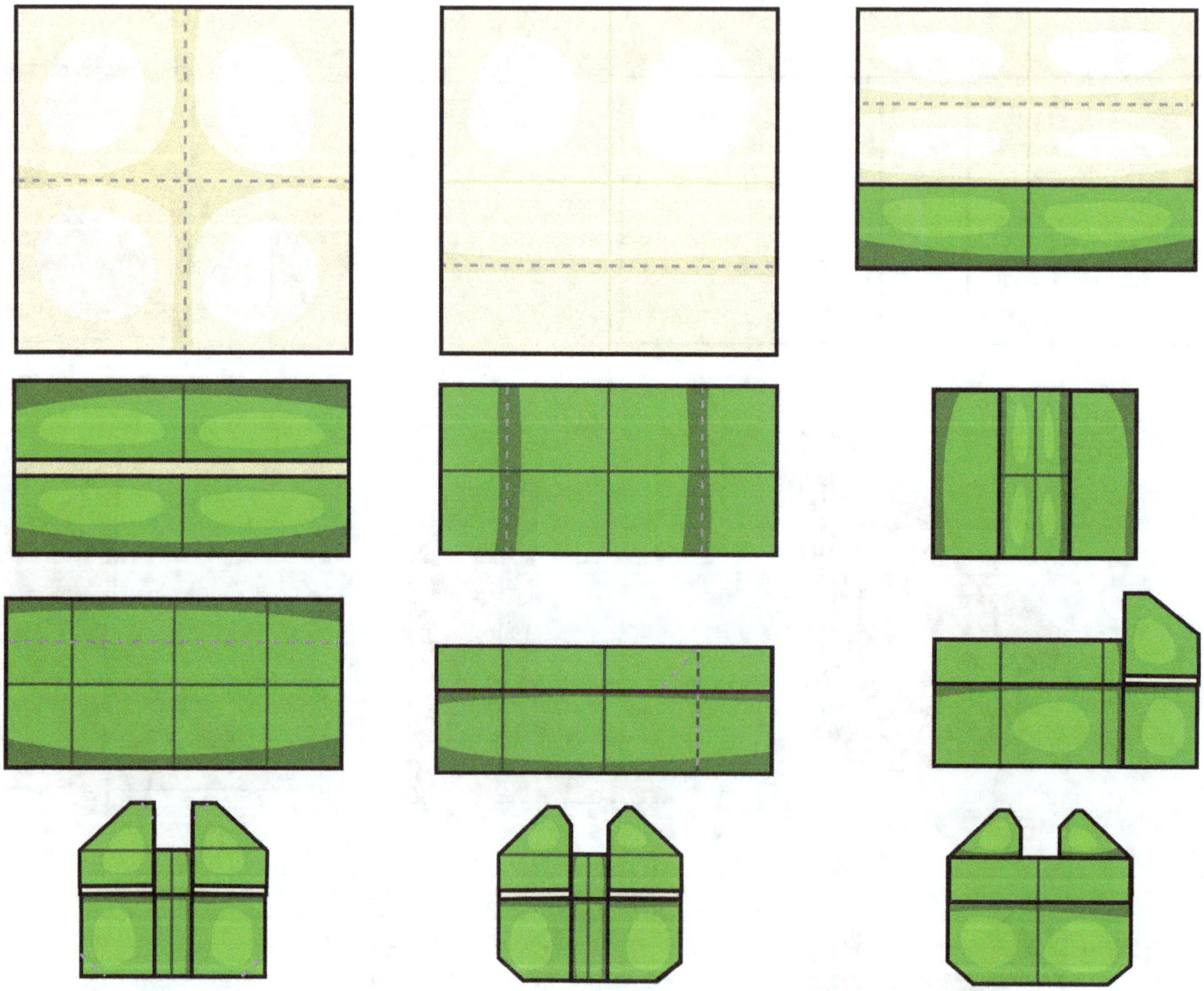

Frog

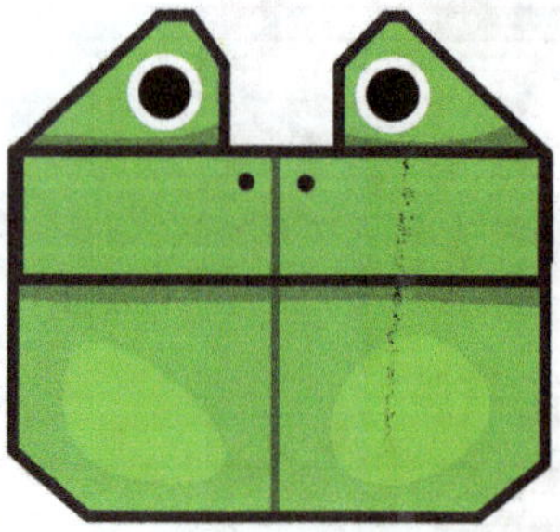

Giraffe

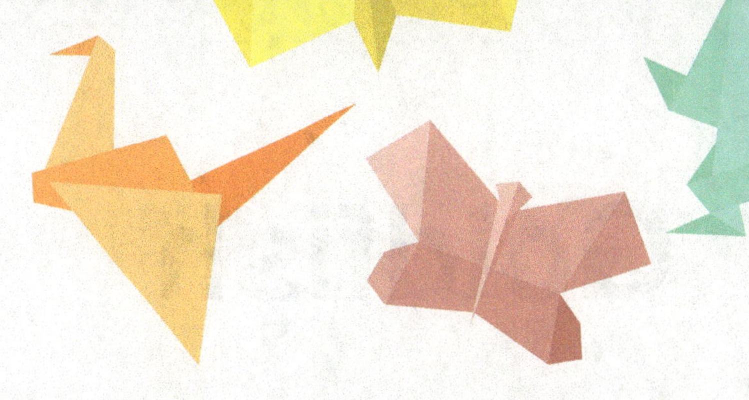

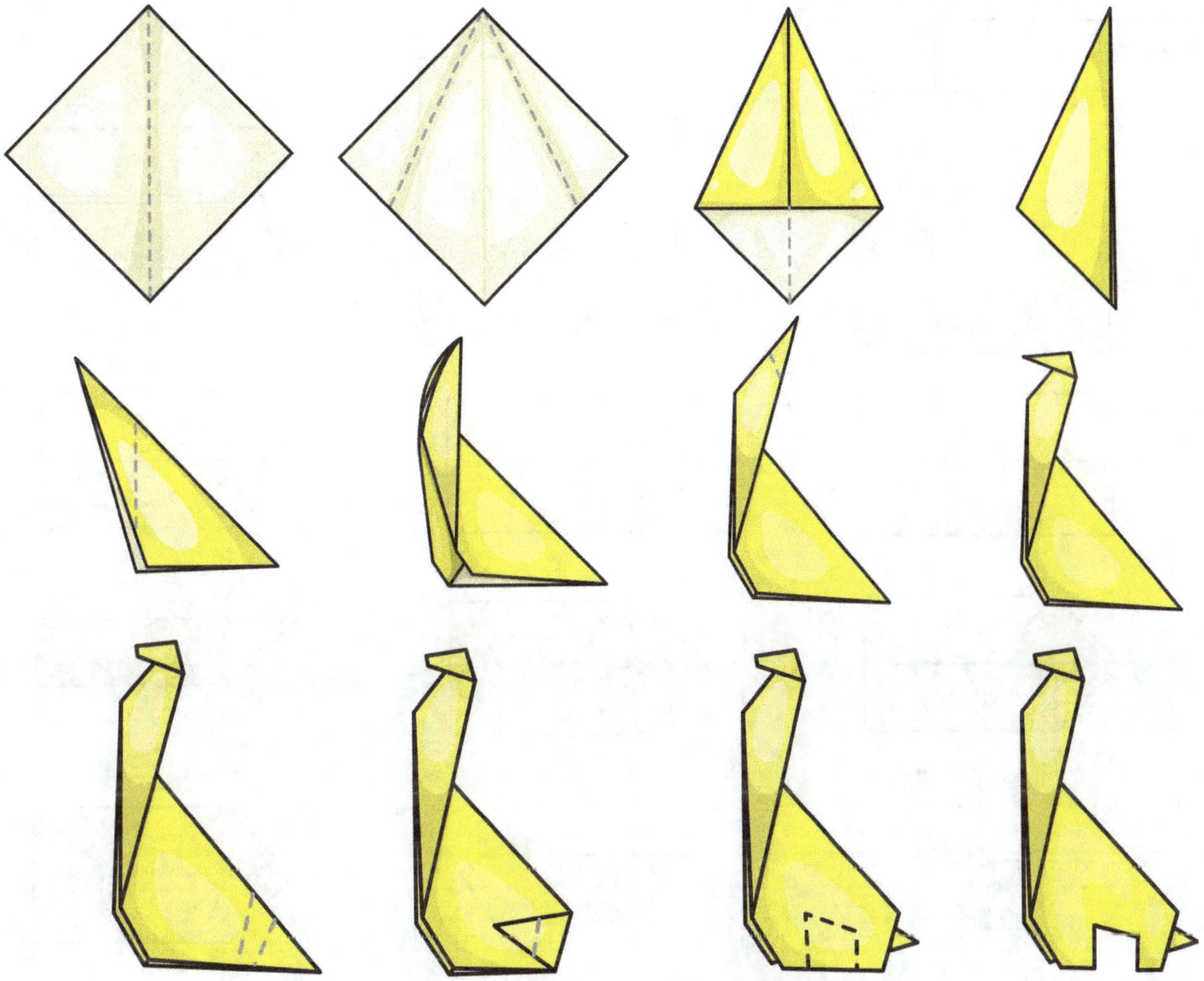

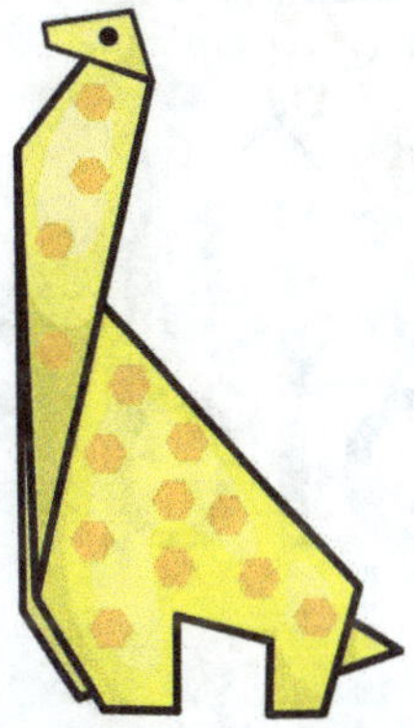

Giraffe

Goldfish

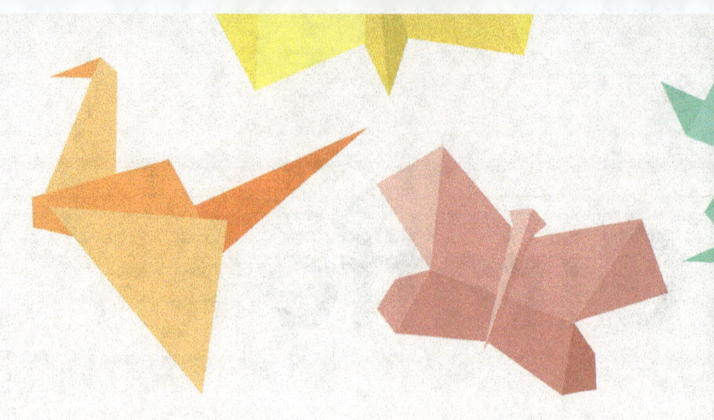

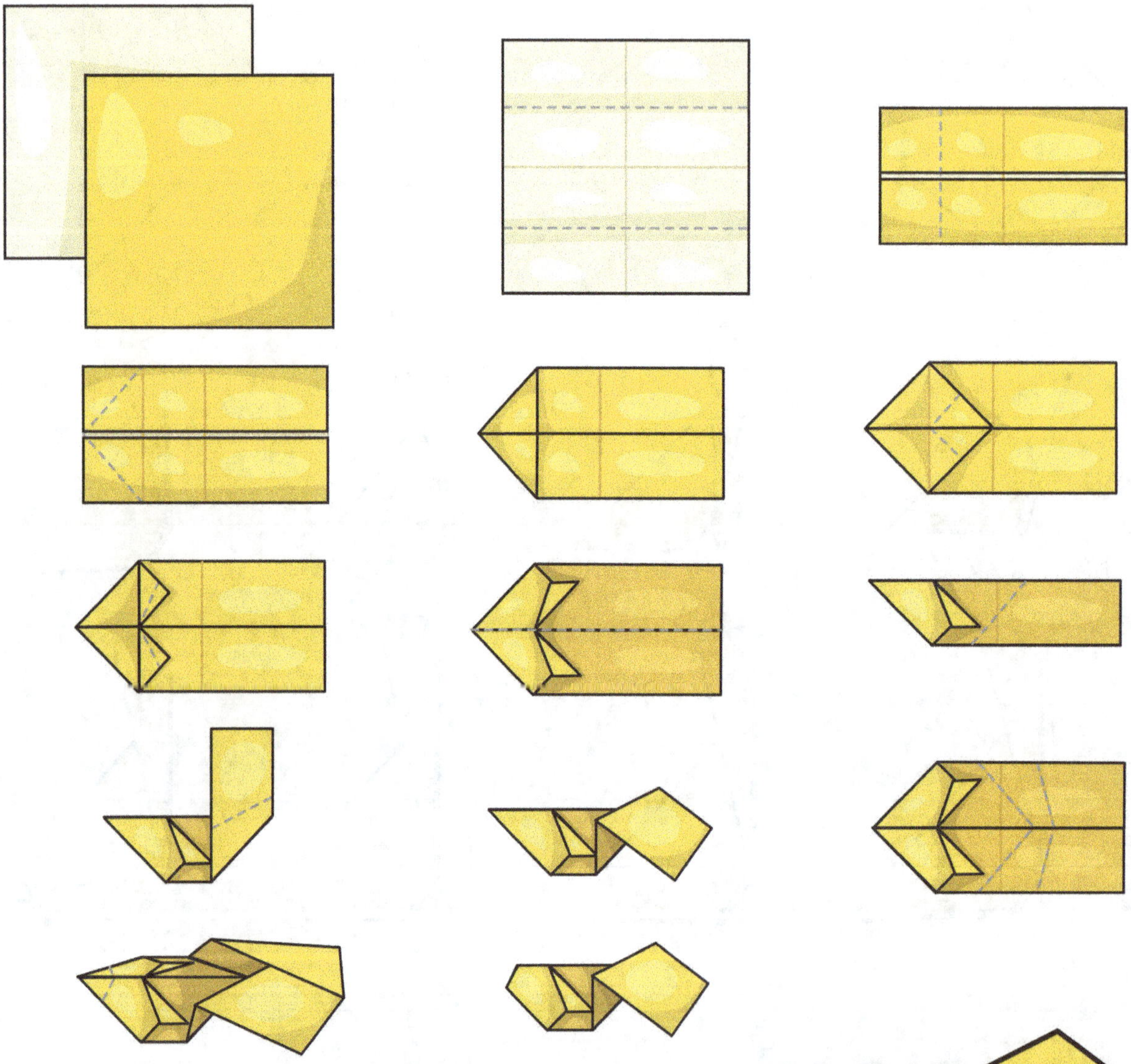

Goldfish

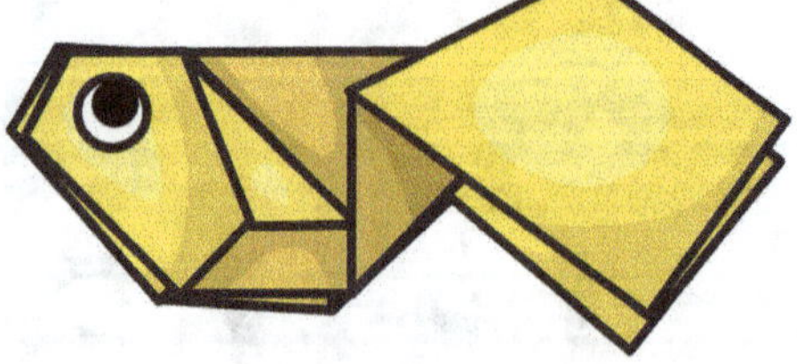

Hamster

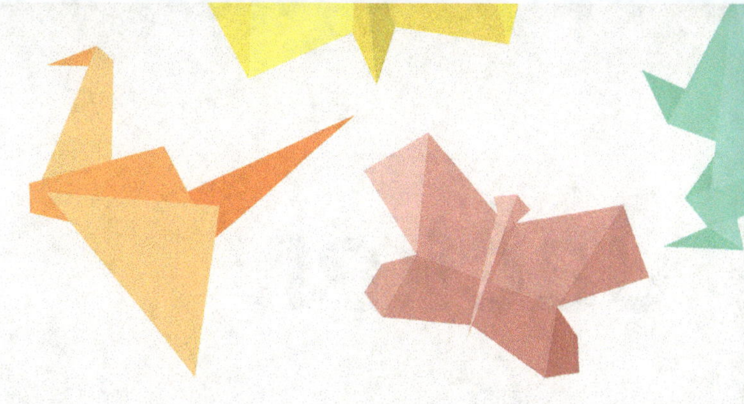

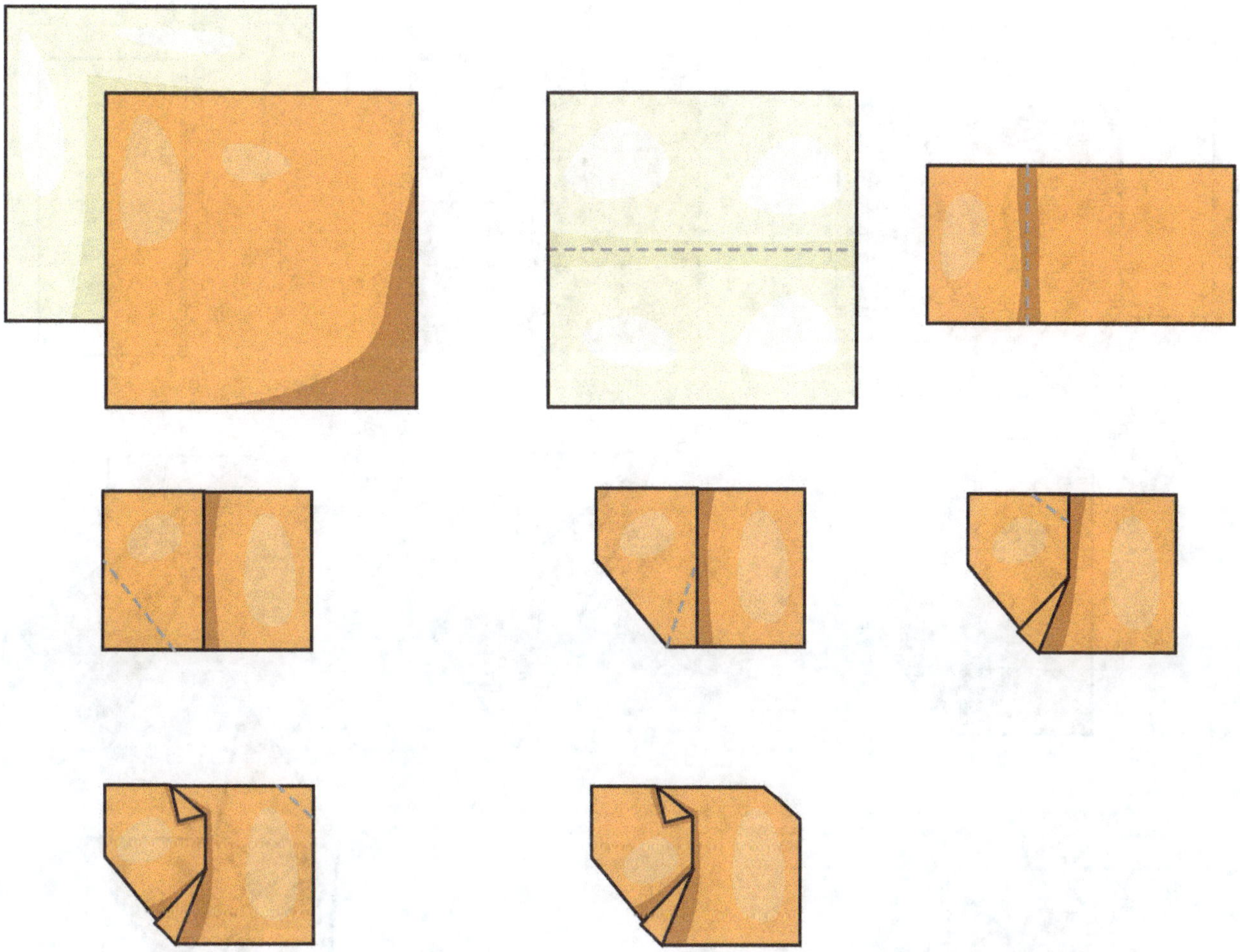

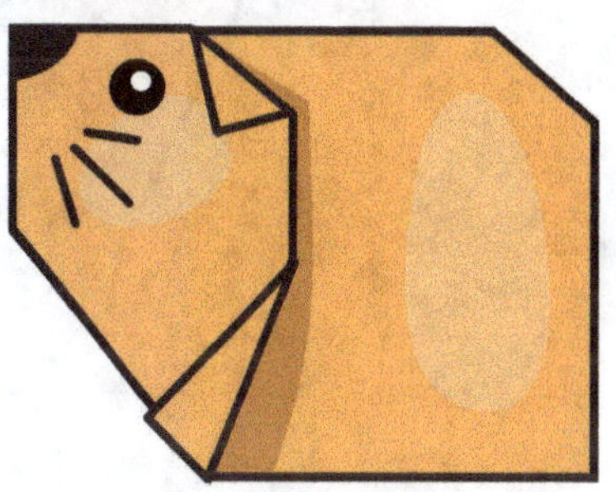

Hamster

Jackal

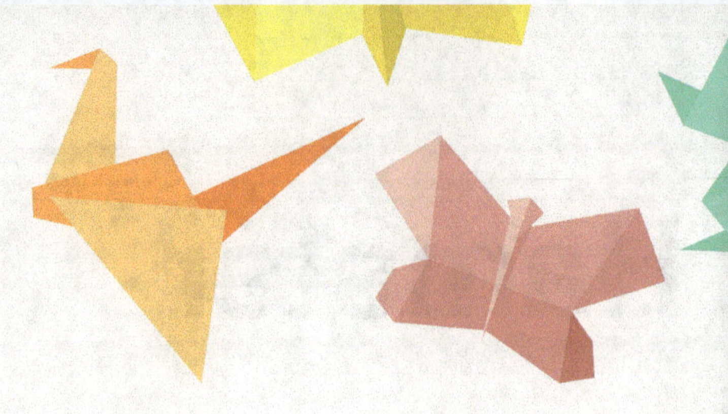

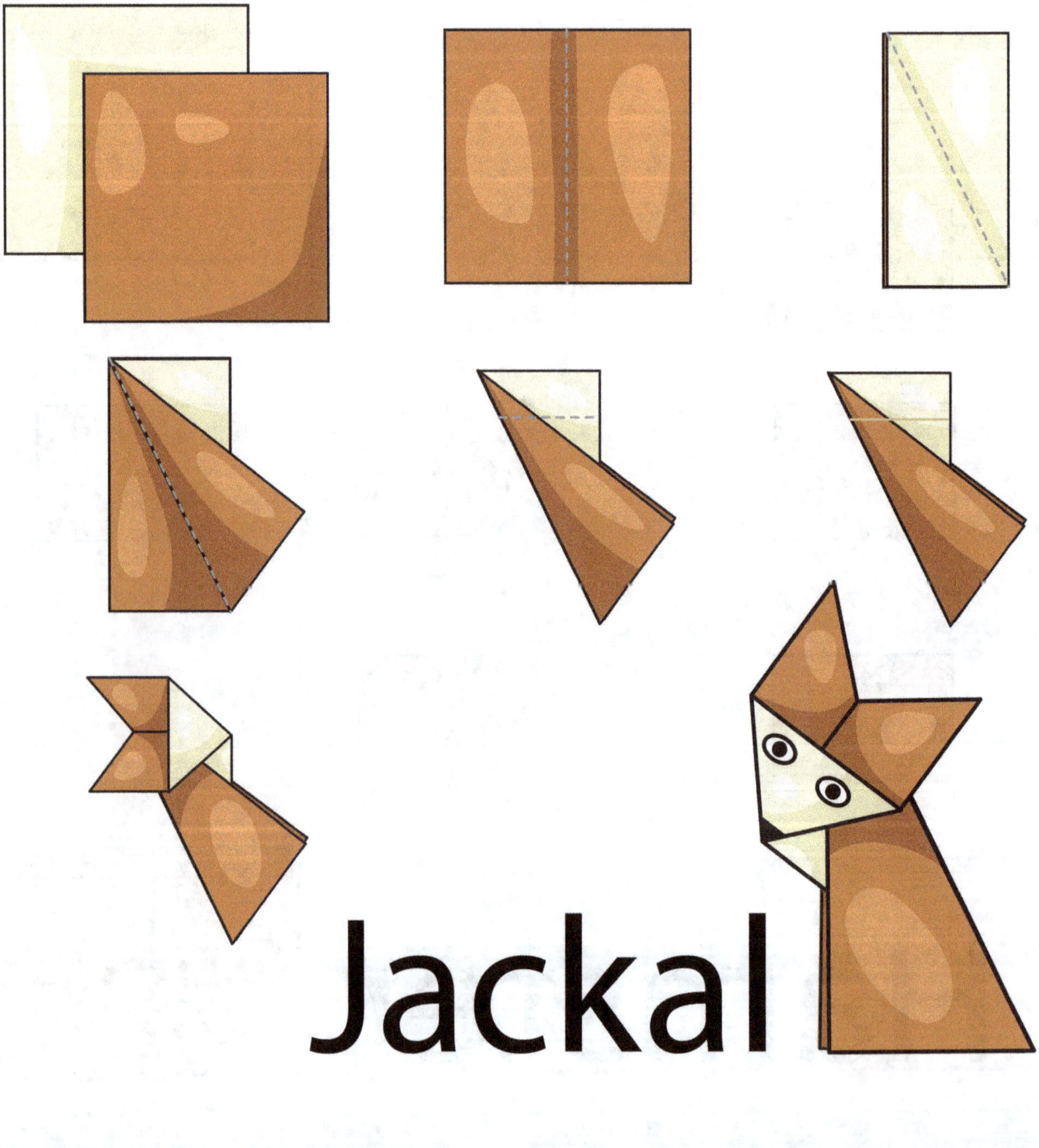

Jackal

Koala

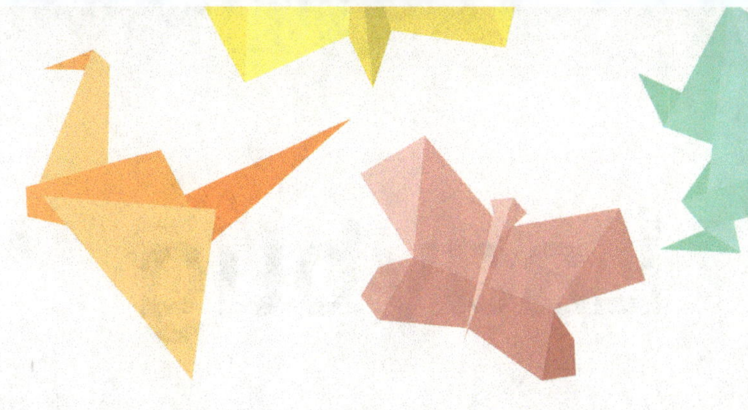

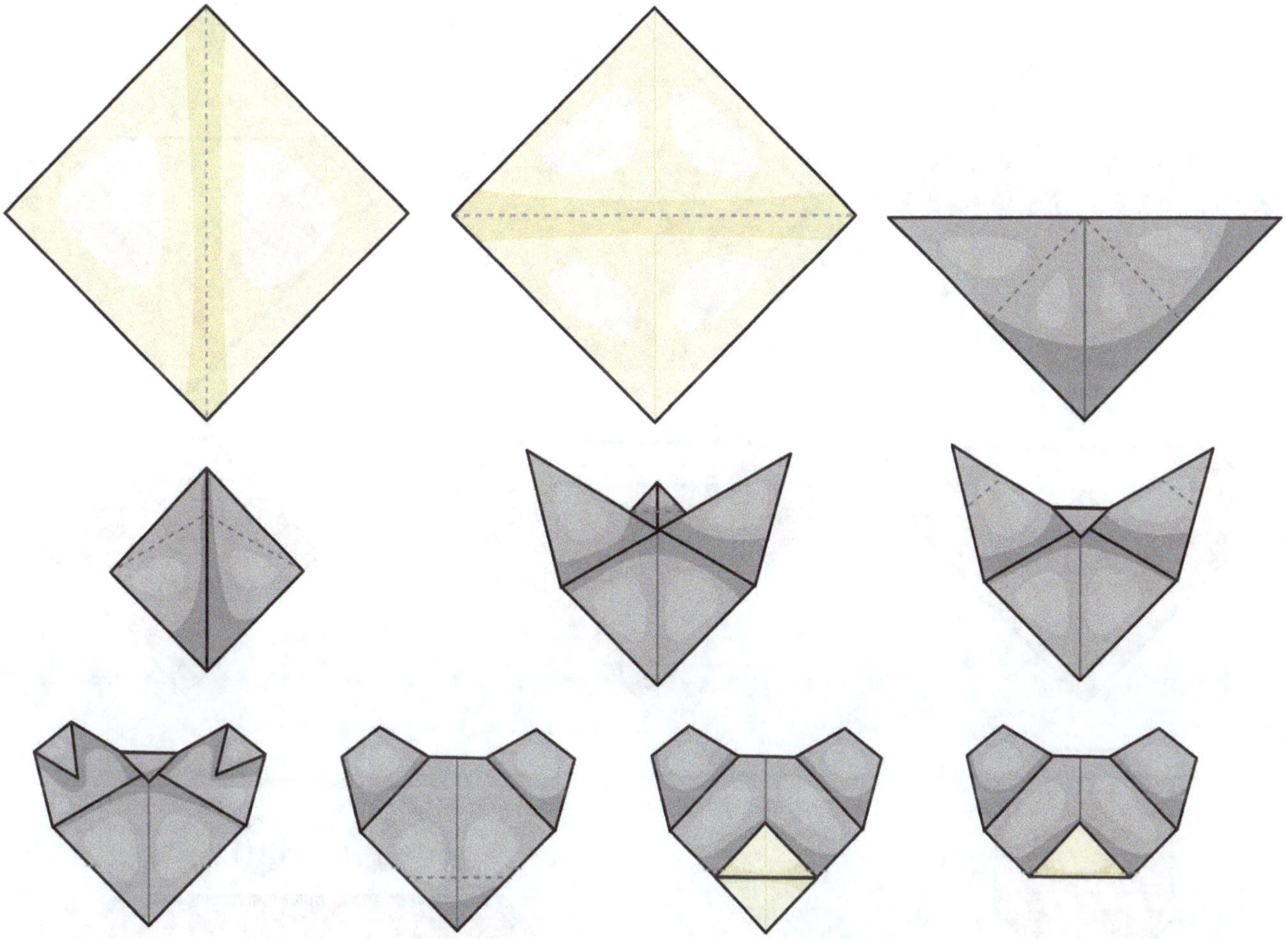

Koala

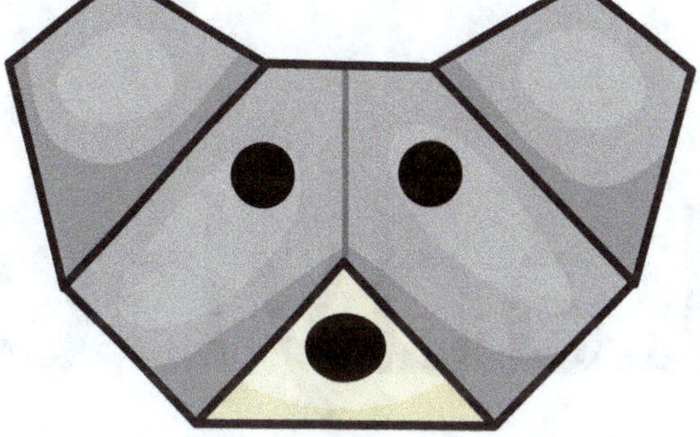

Ladybug

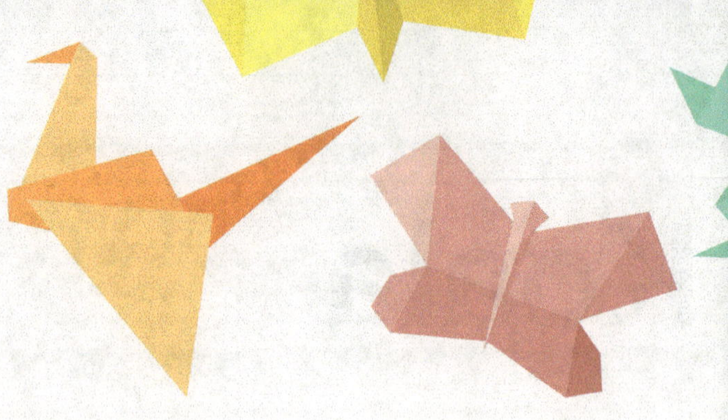

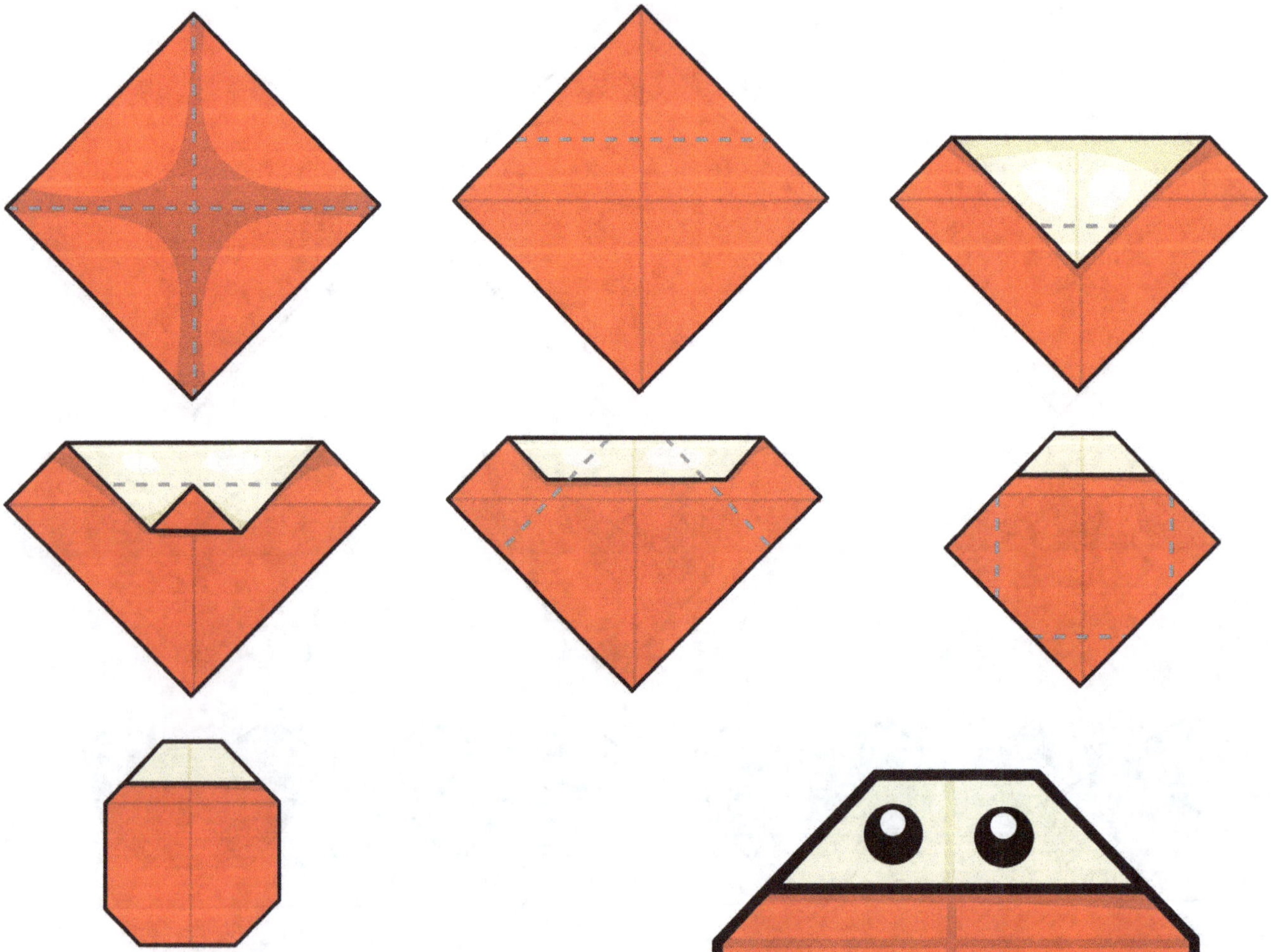

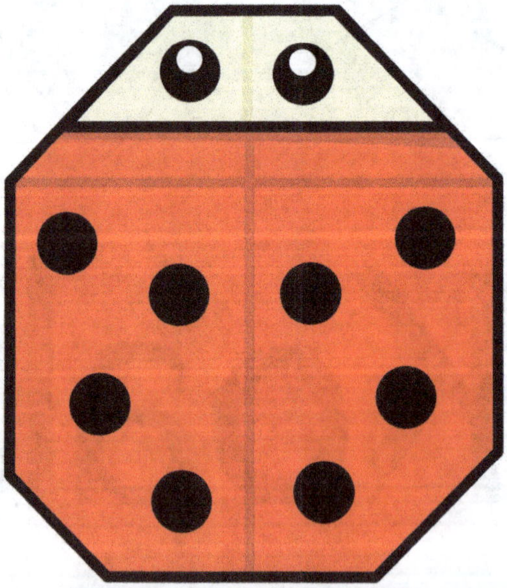

Ladybug

Monkey

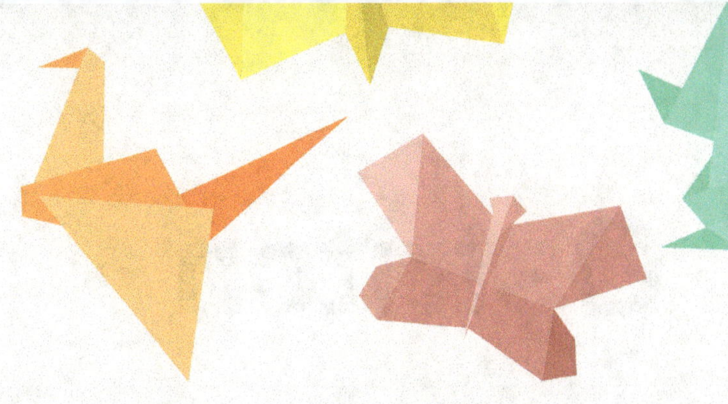

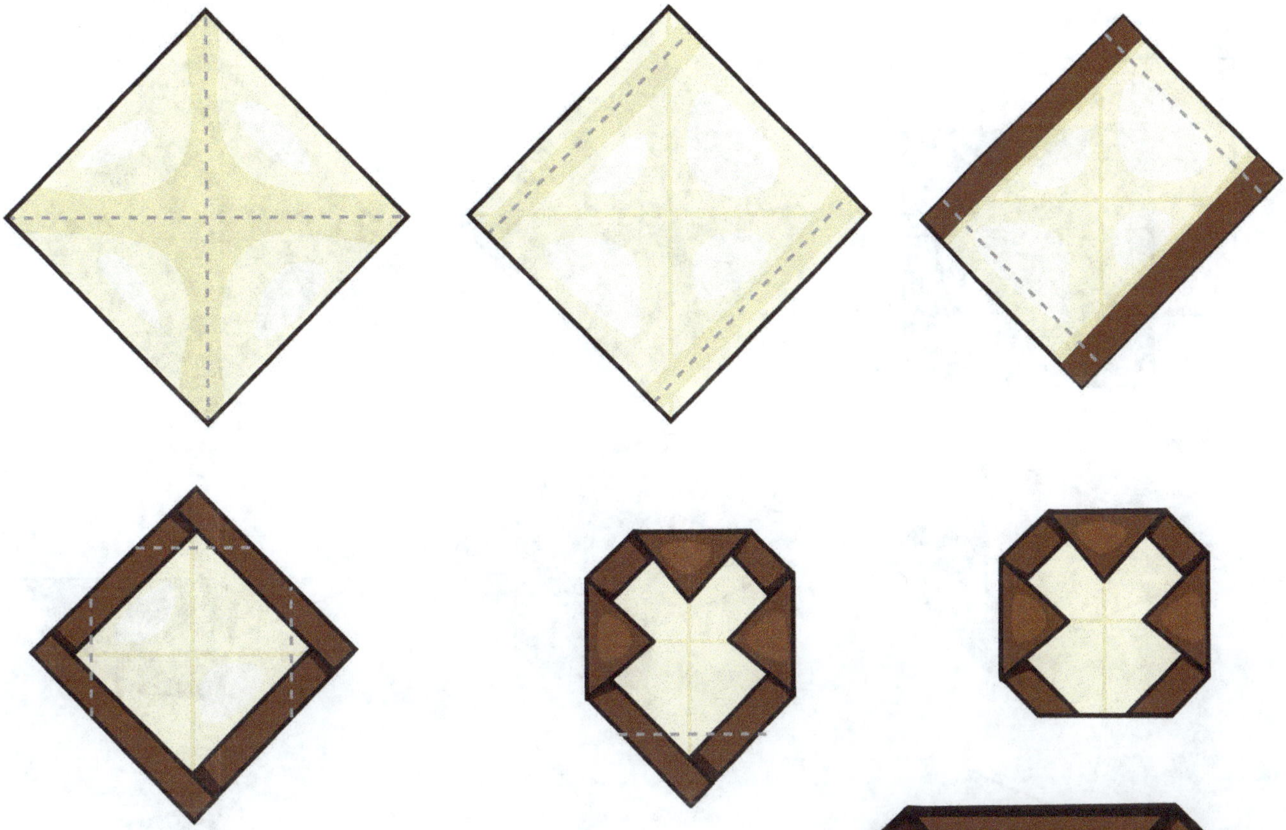

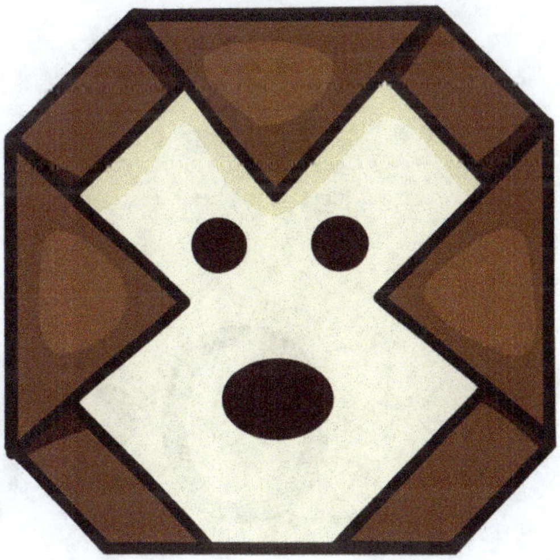

Monkey

Ostritch

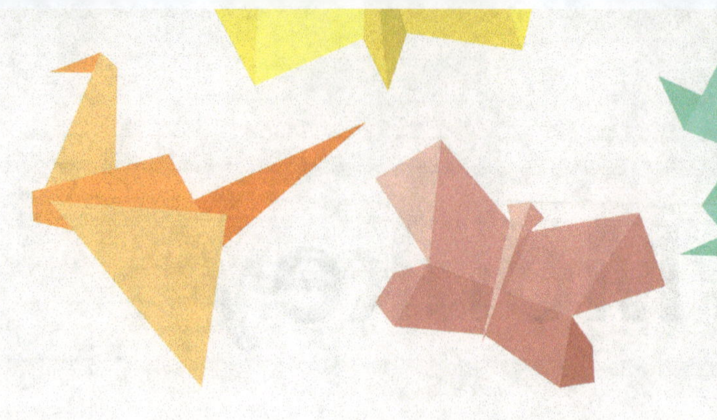

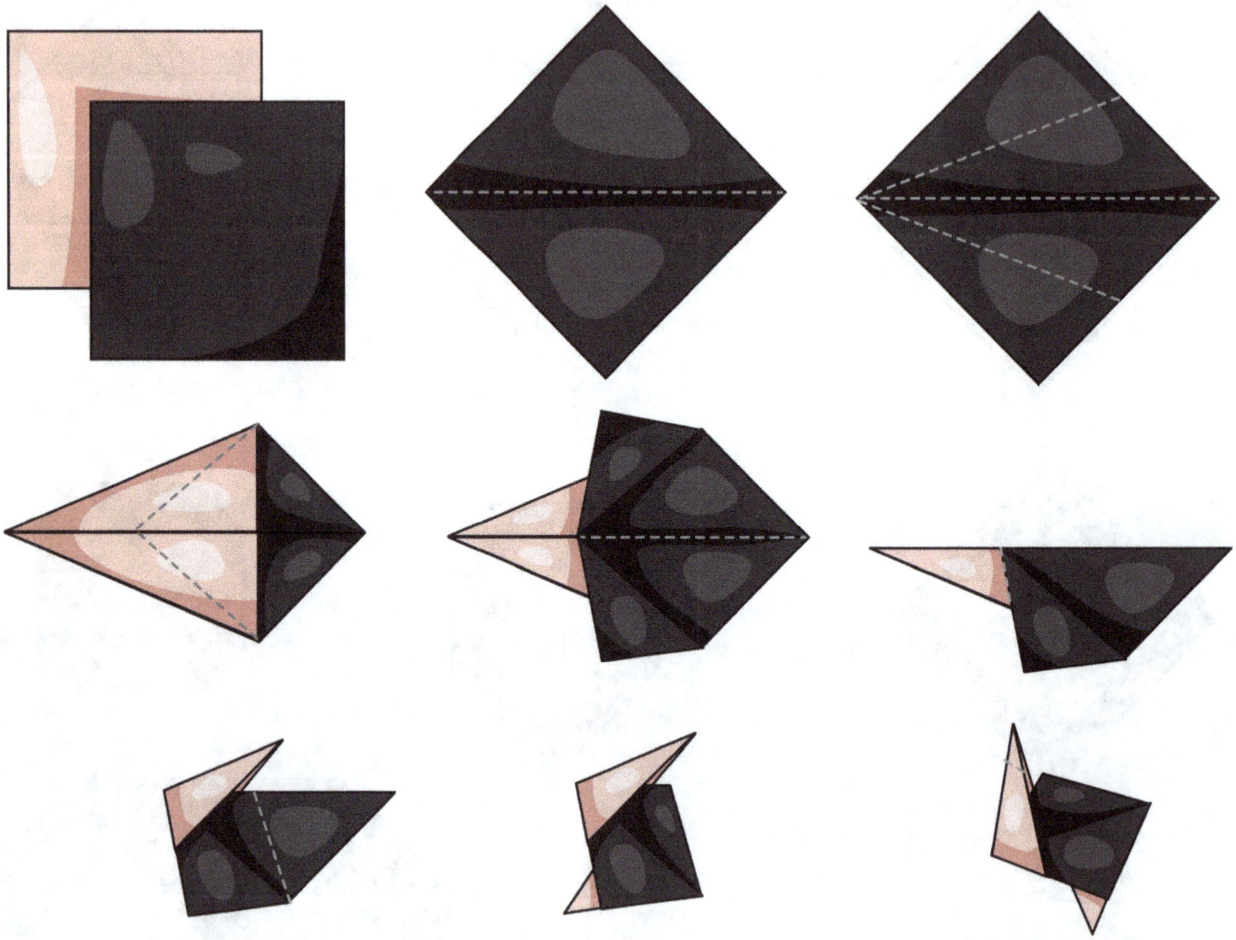

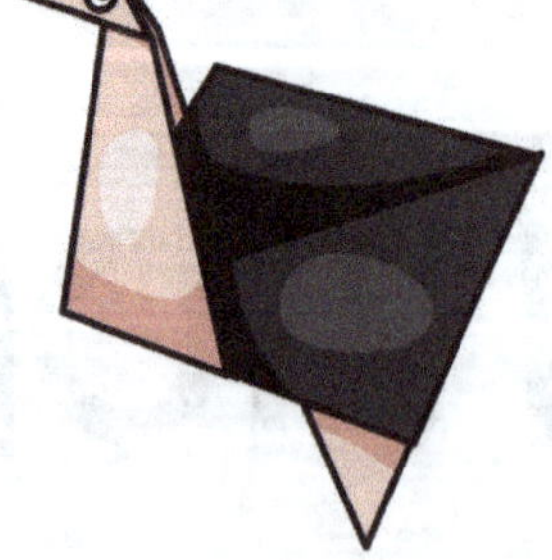

Ostrich

Panda

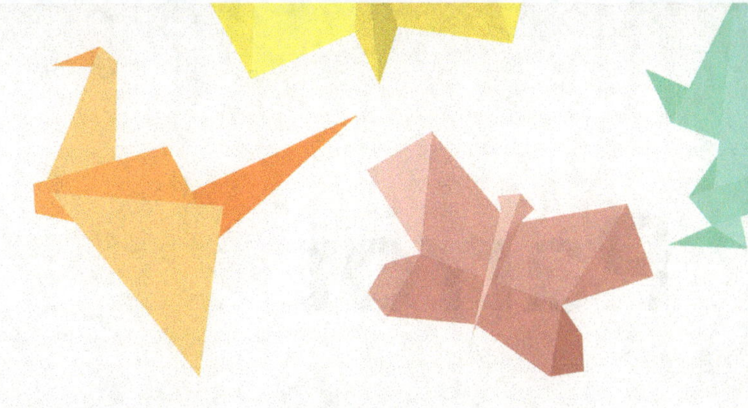

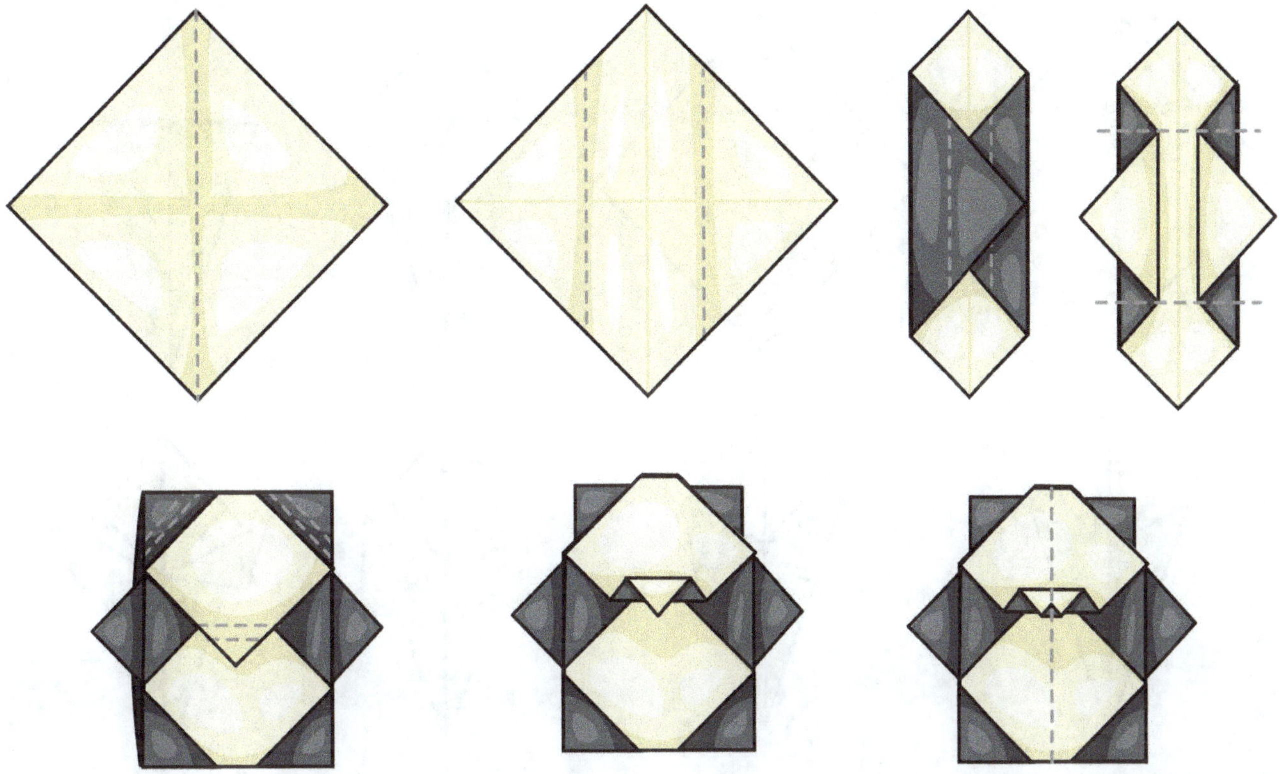

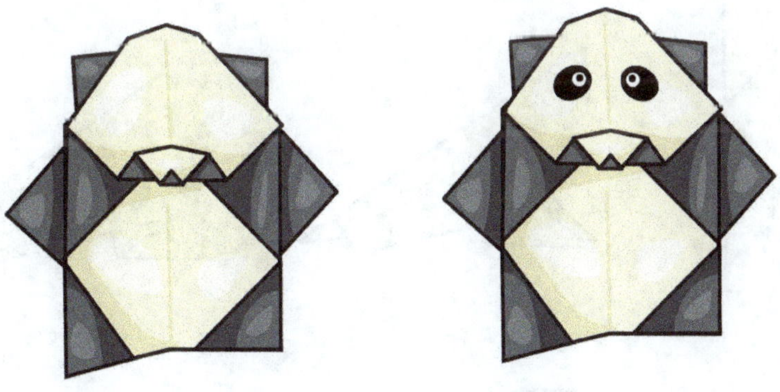

Panda

Parrot

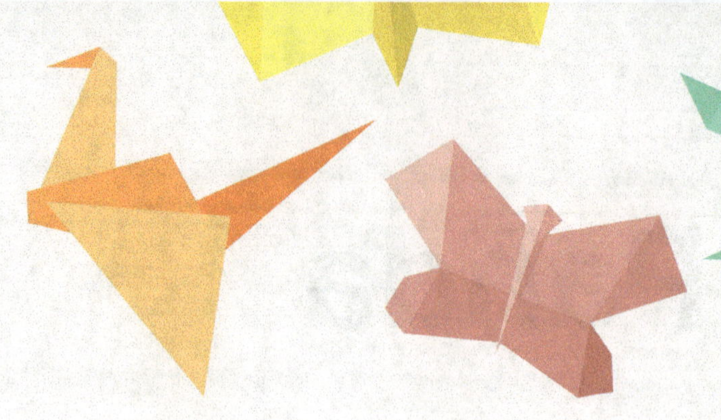

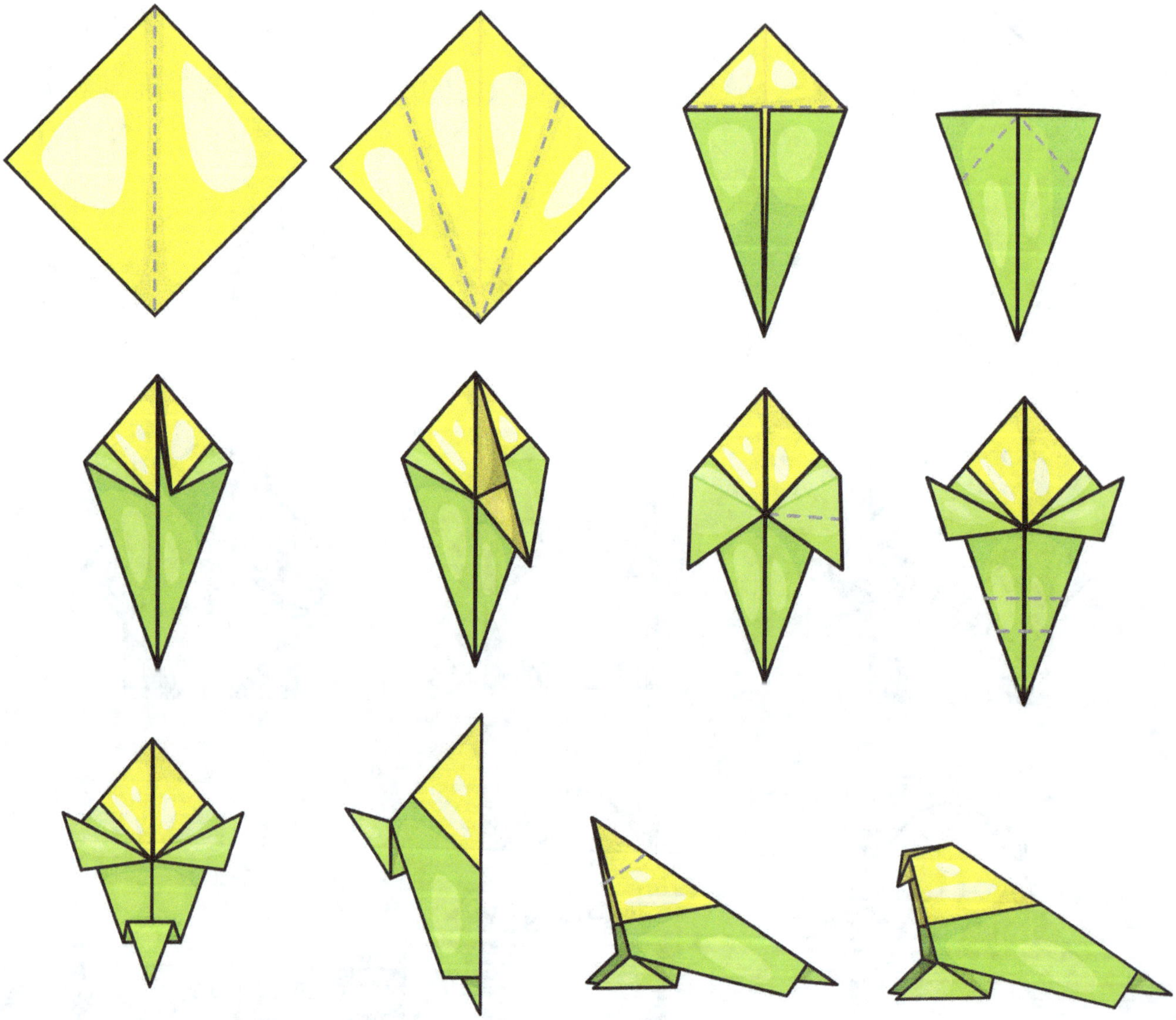

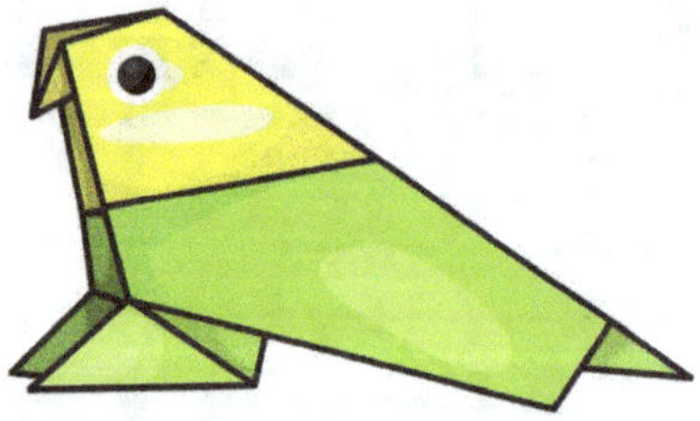

Parrot

Peacock

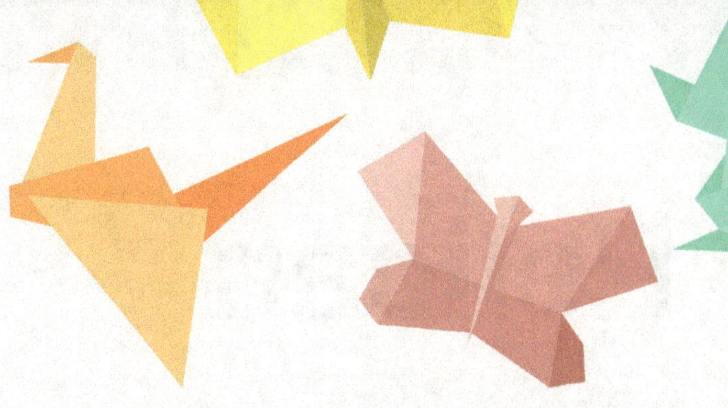

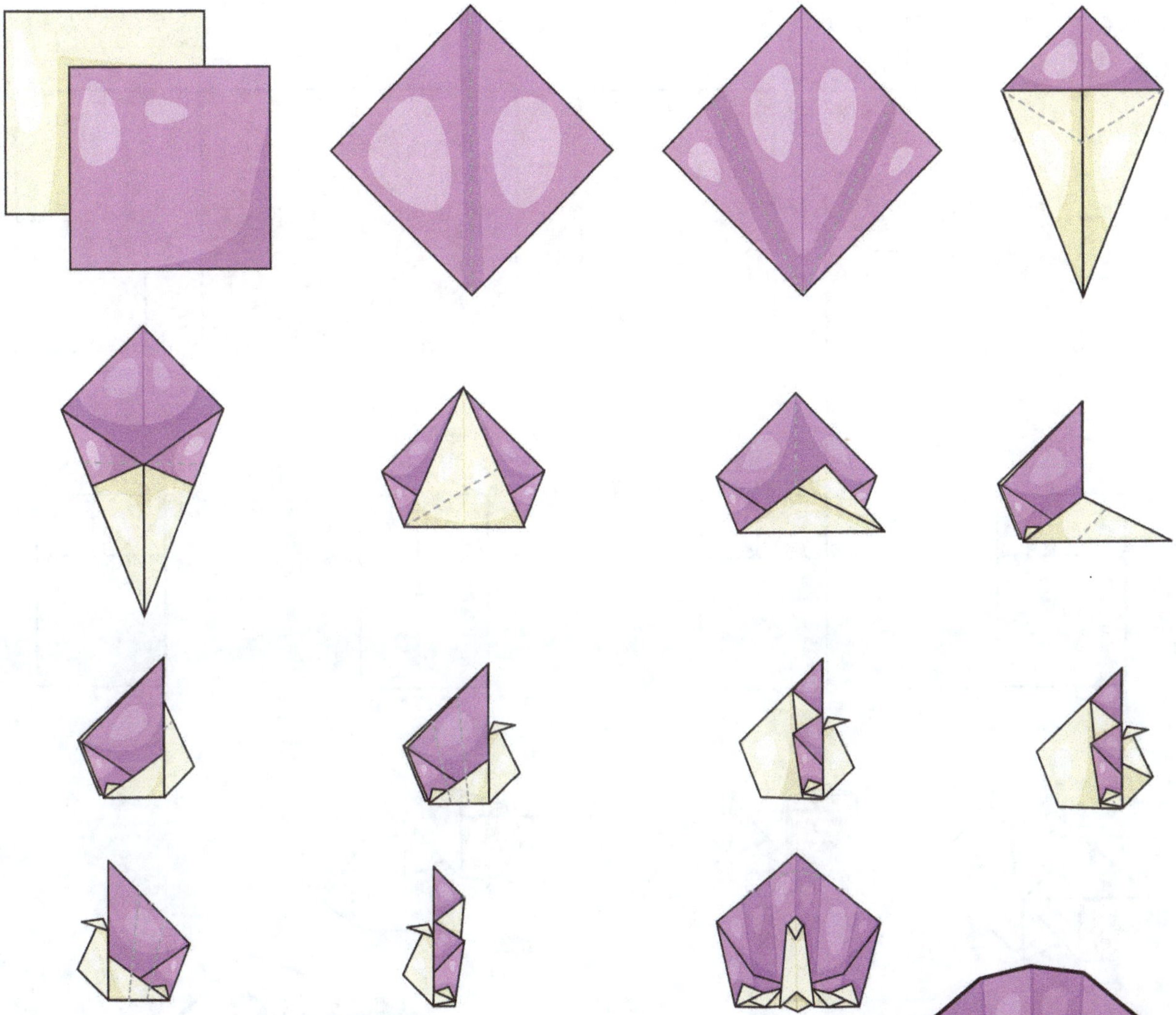

Peacock

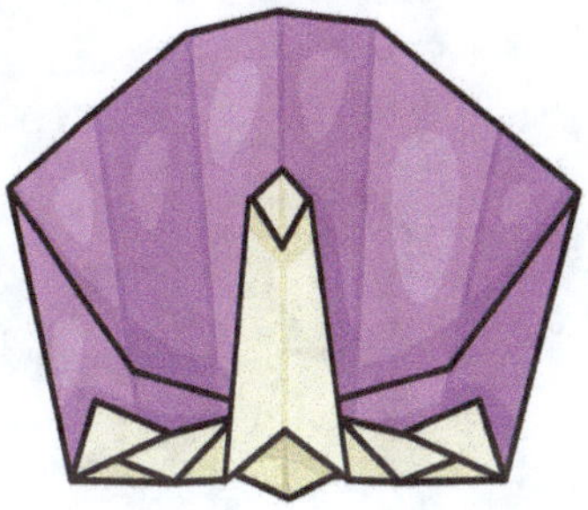

Pelican

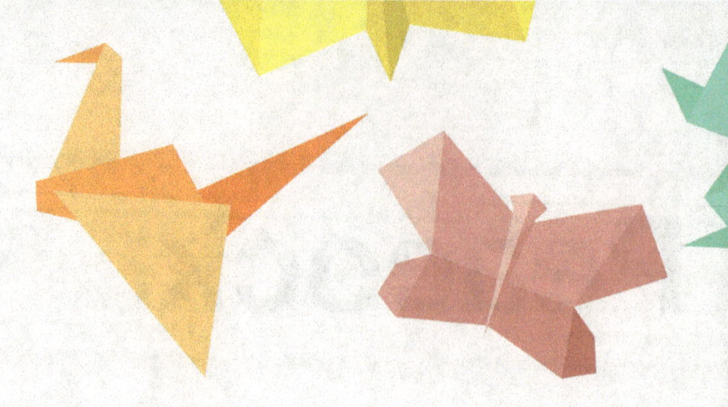

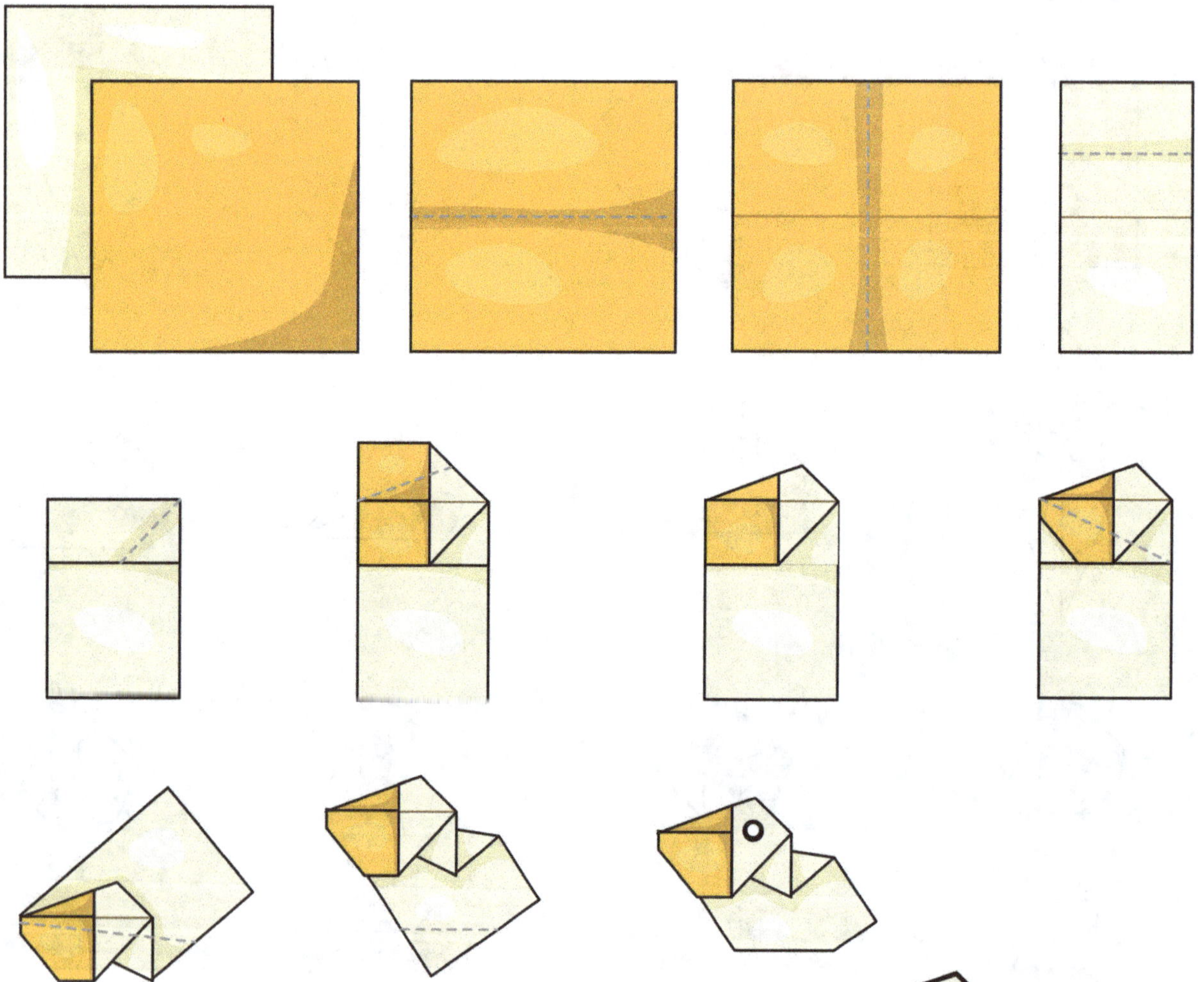

Pelican

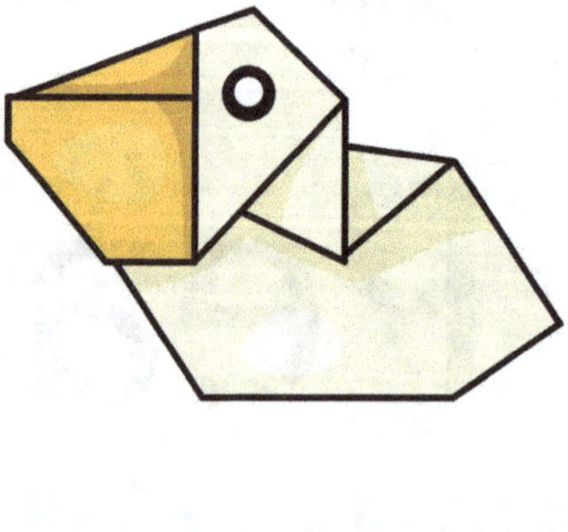

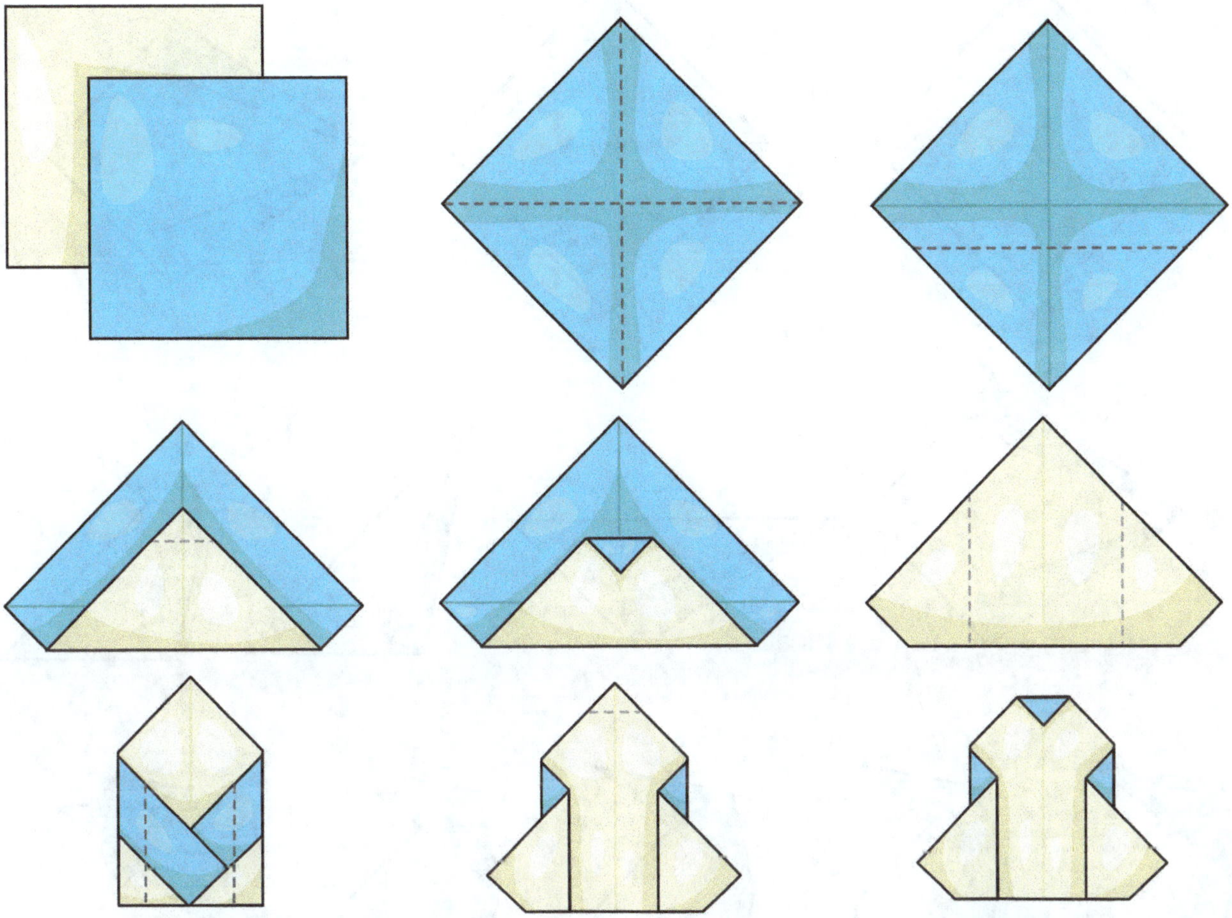

Penguin

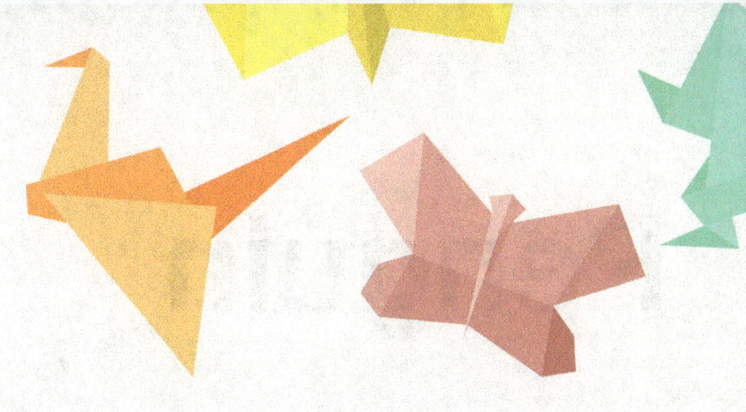

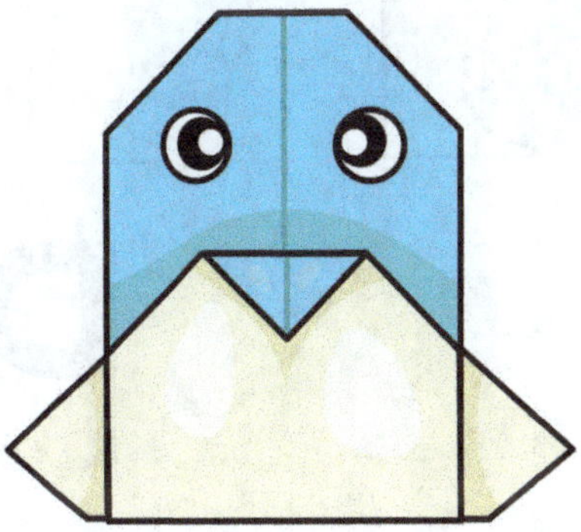

Penguin

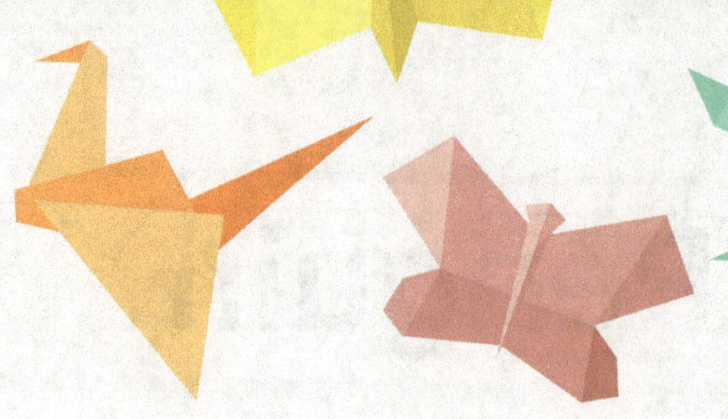

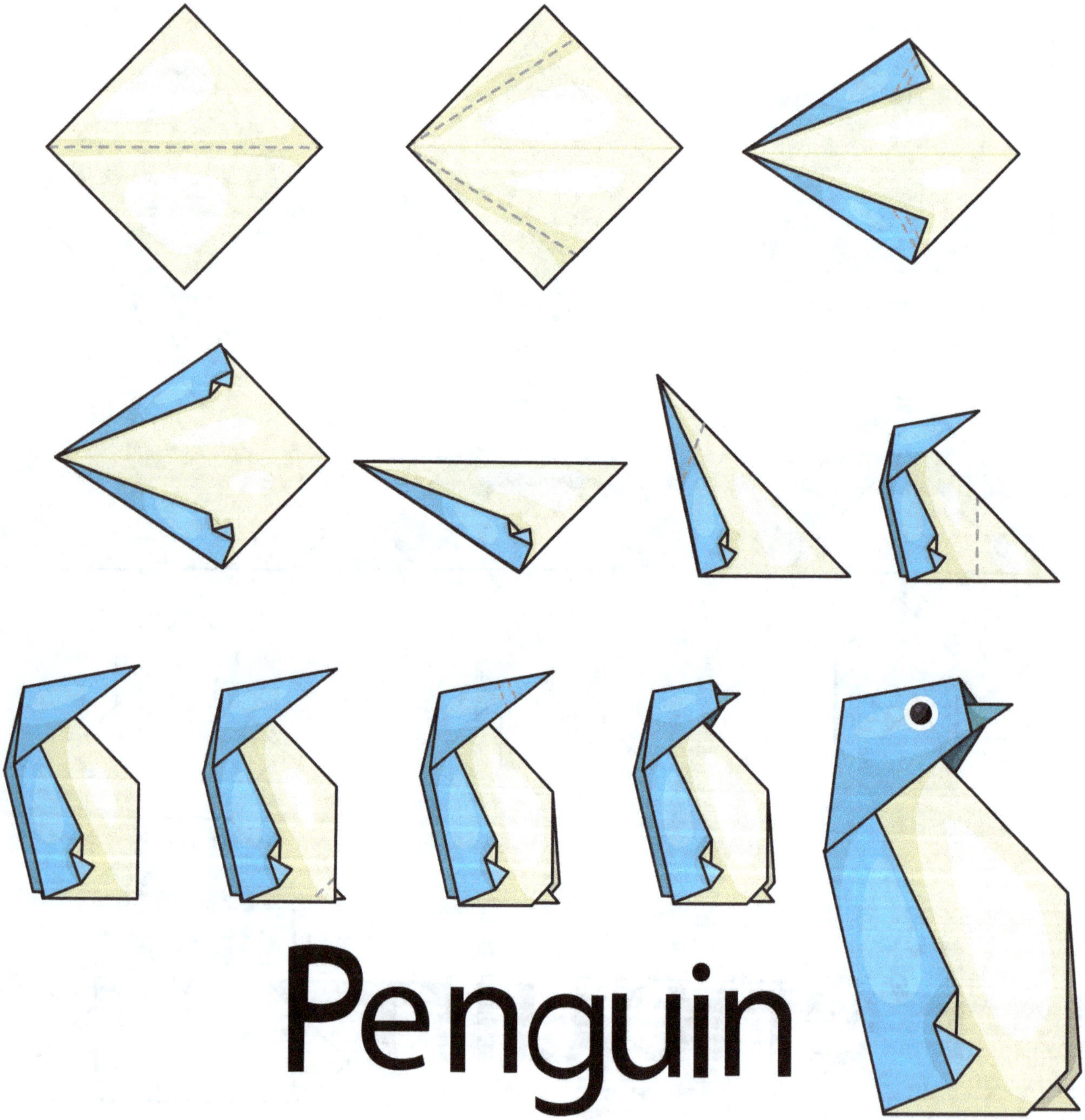

Penguin

Pig

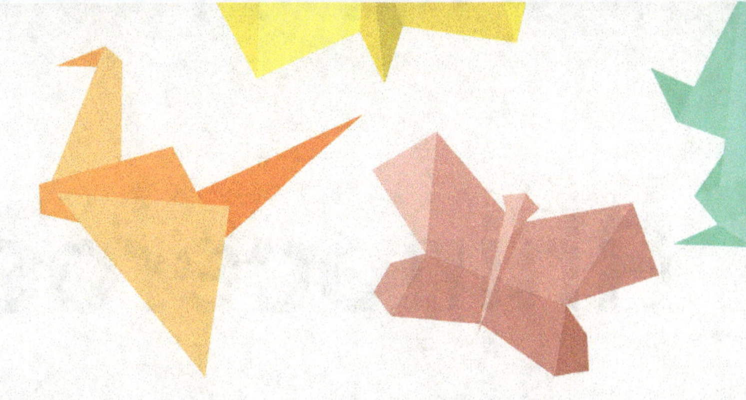

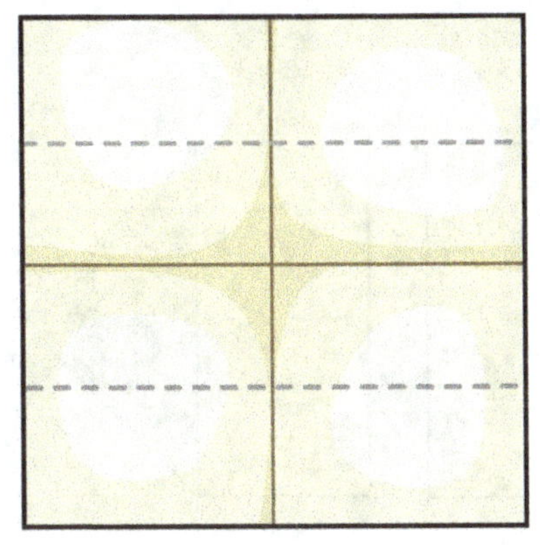
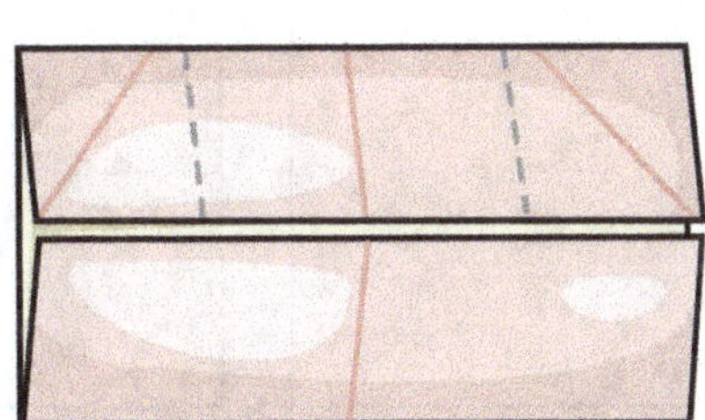
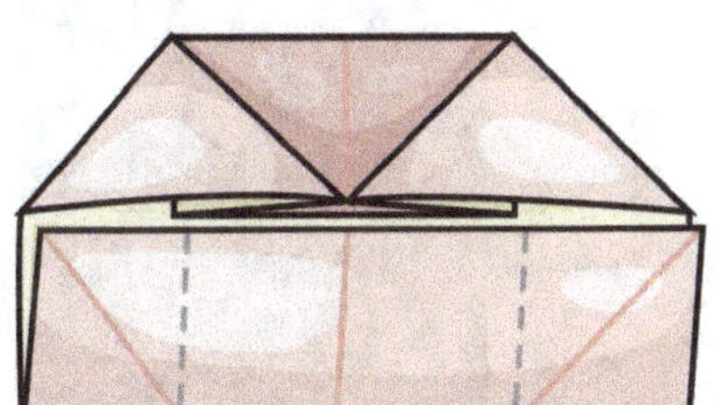

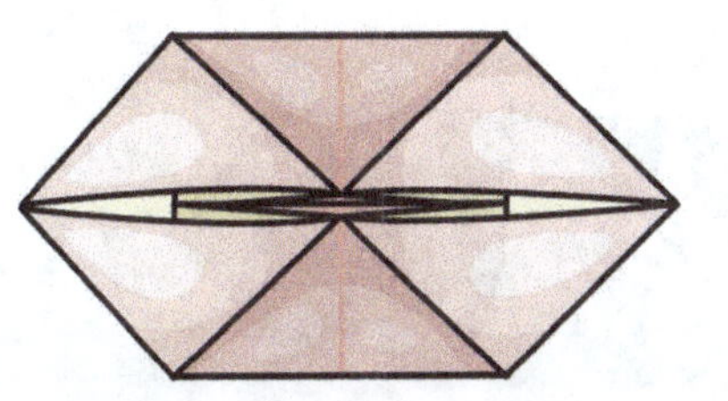
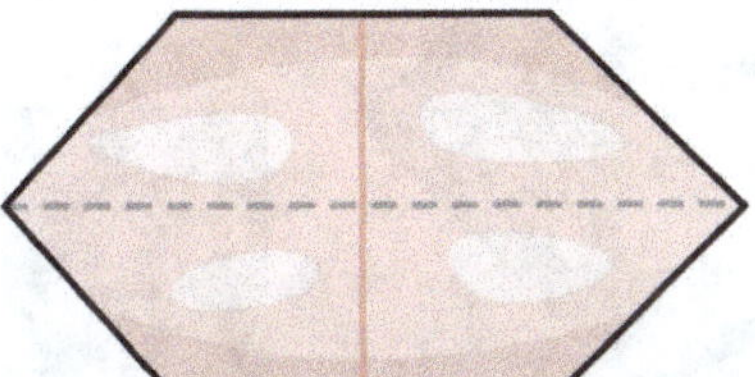
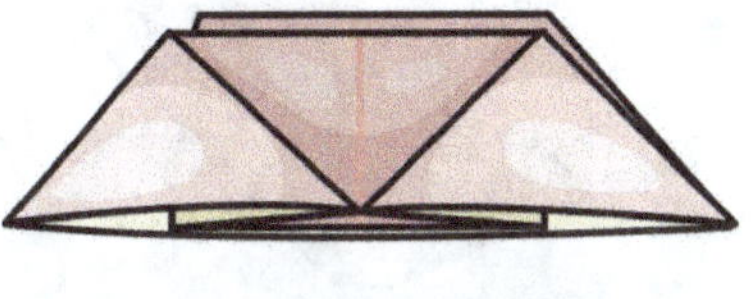

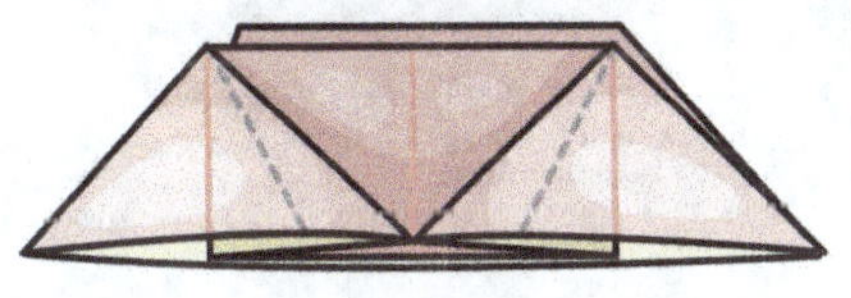
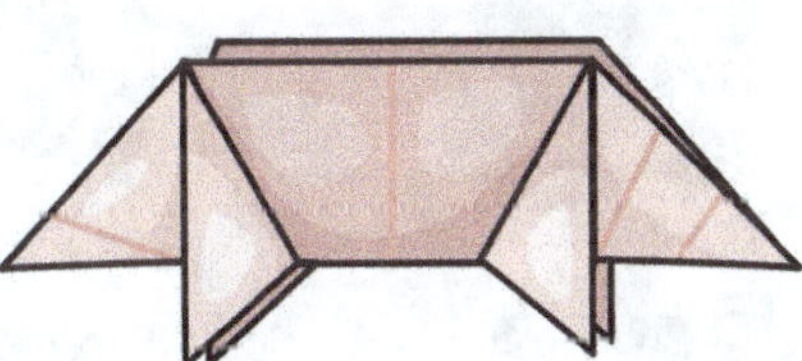
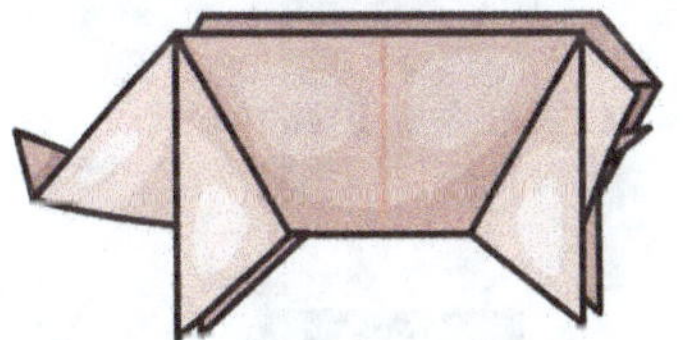

Pig

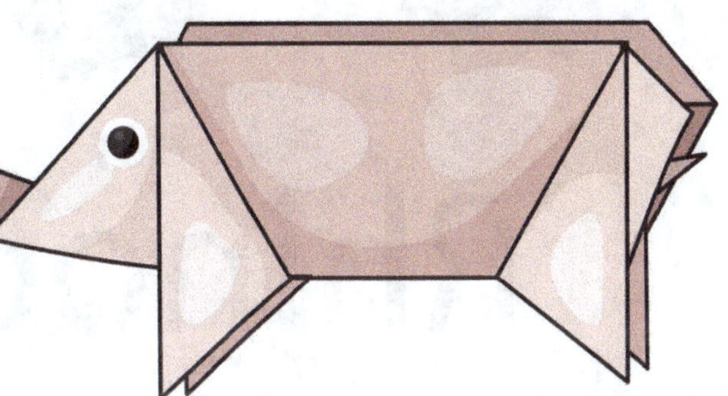

Rhinoceros

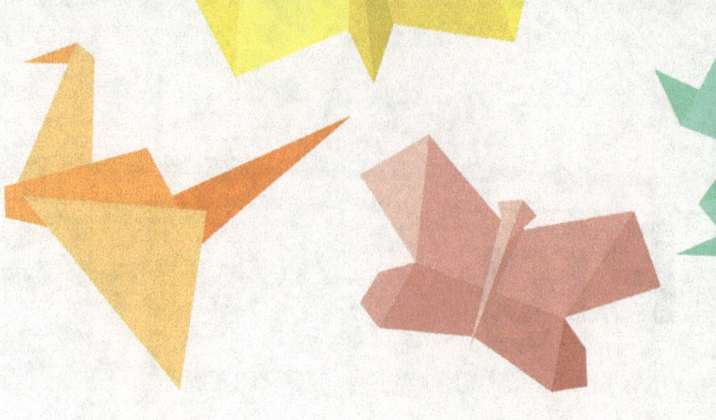

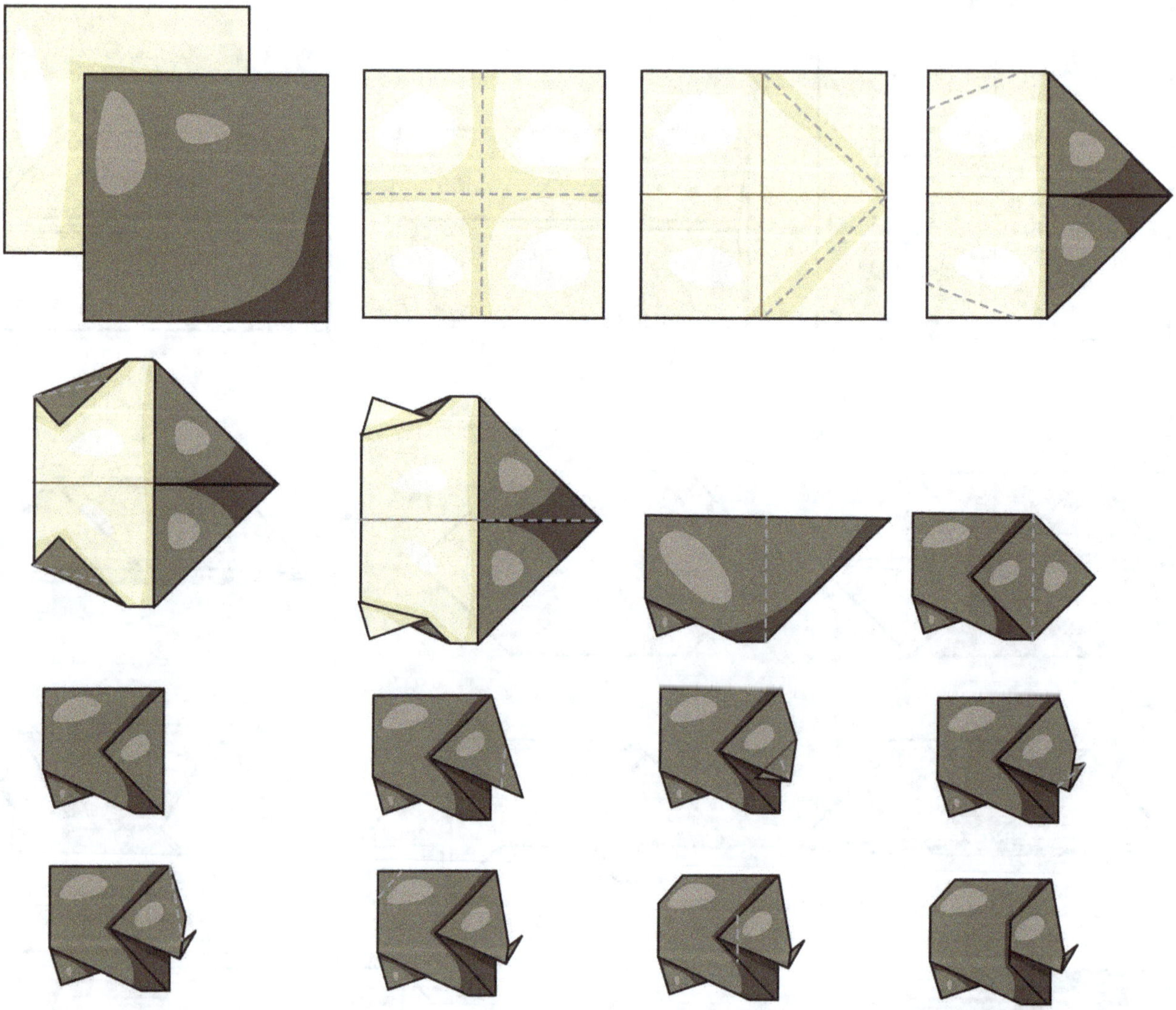

Rhinoceros

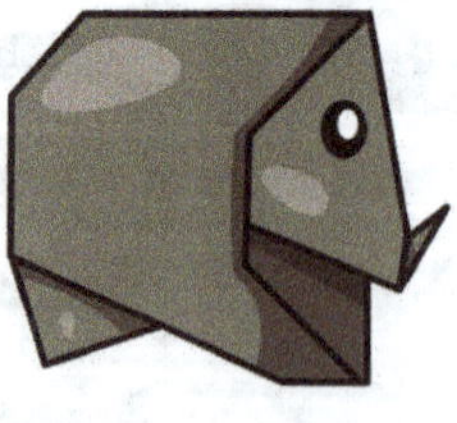

Ship

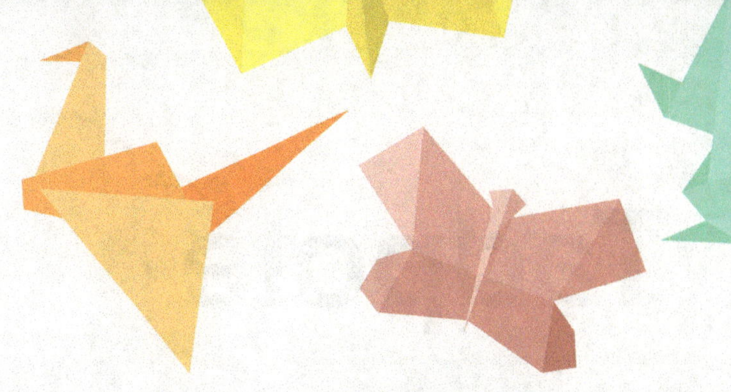

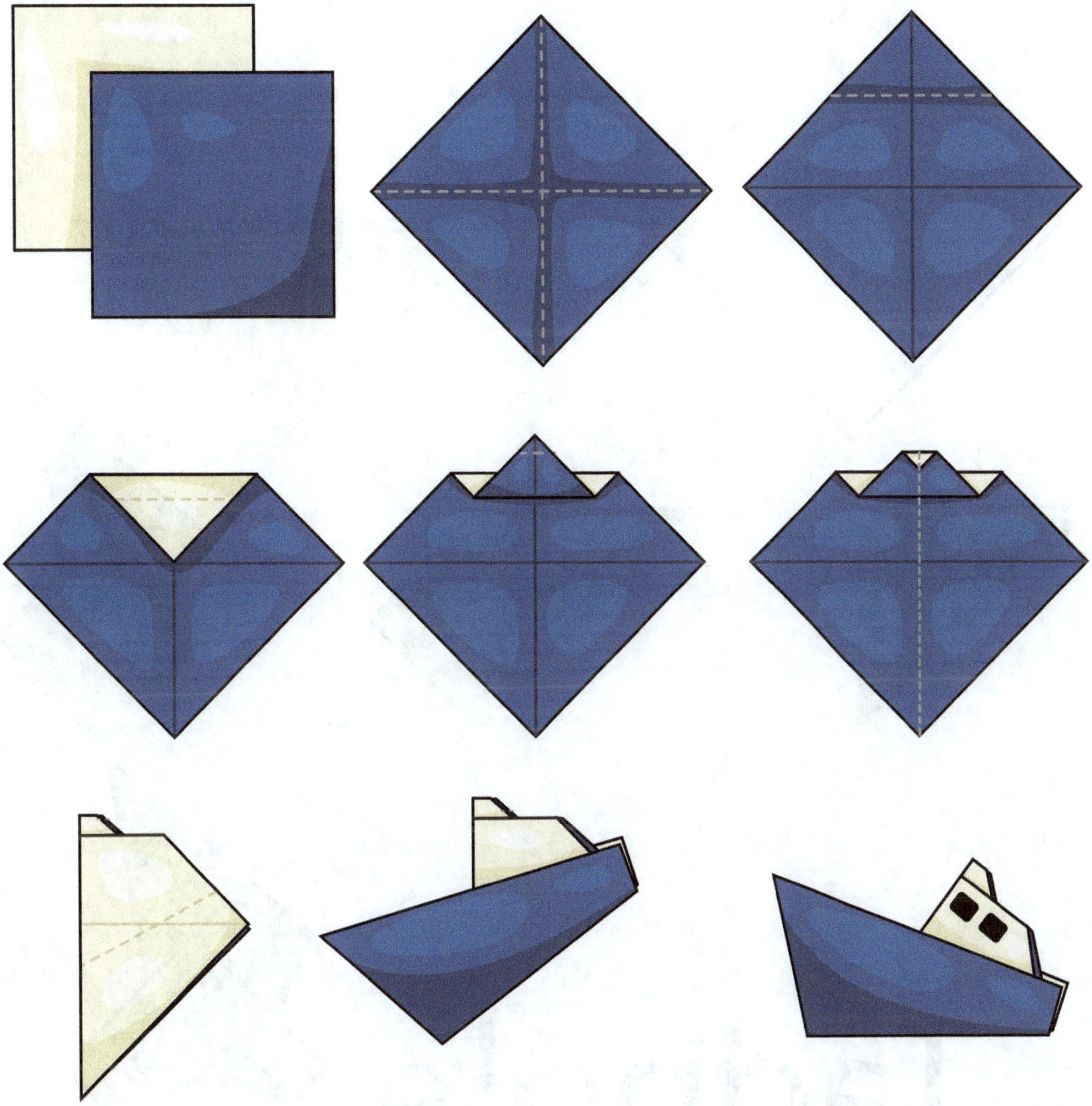

Tadpole

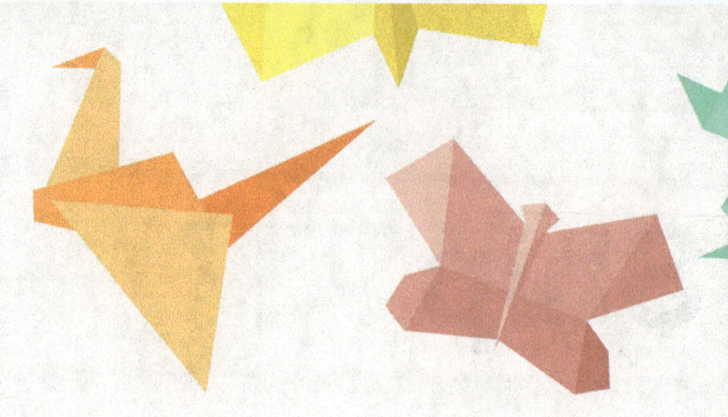

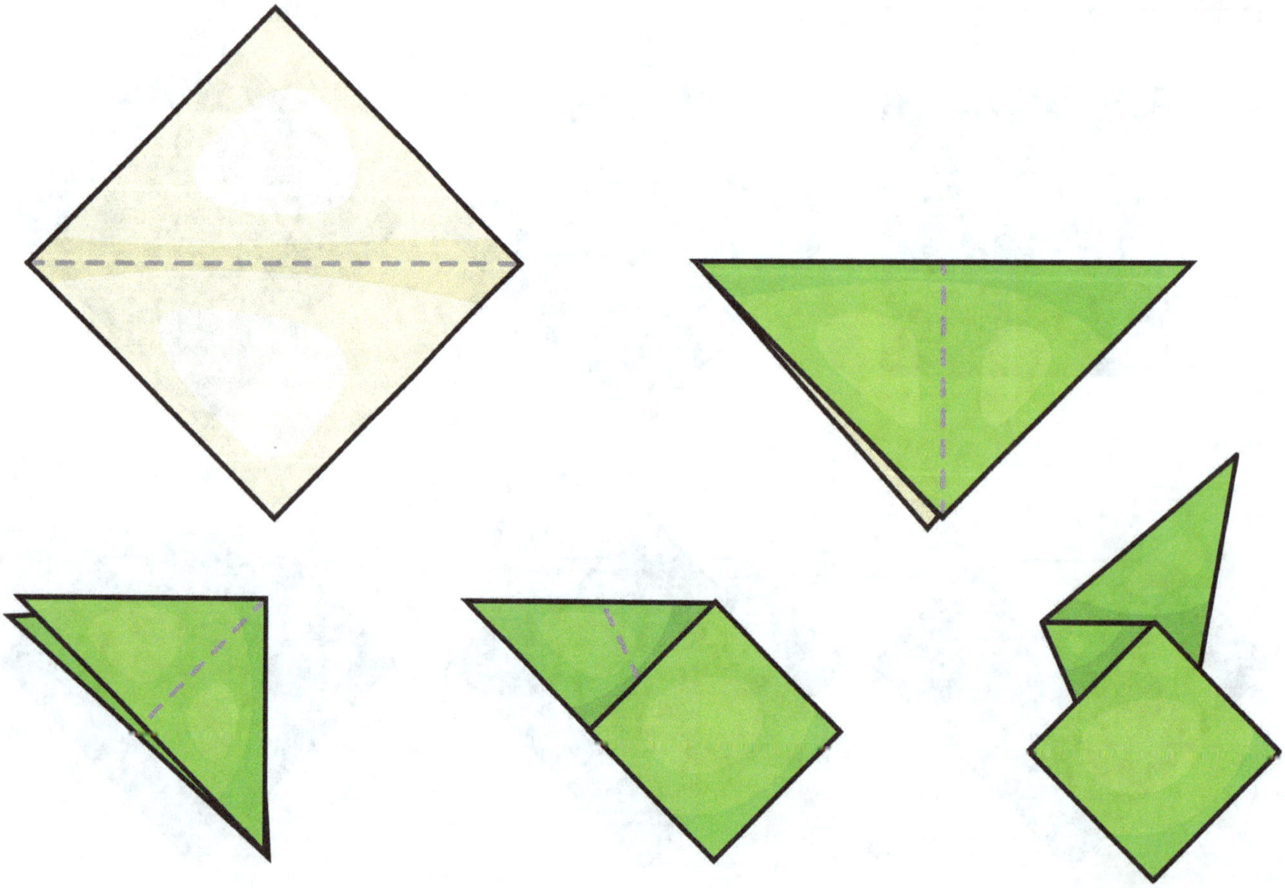

Tadpole

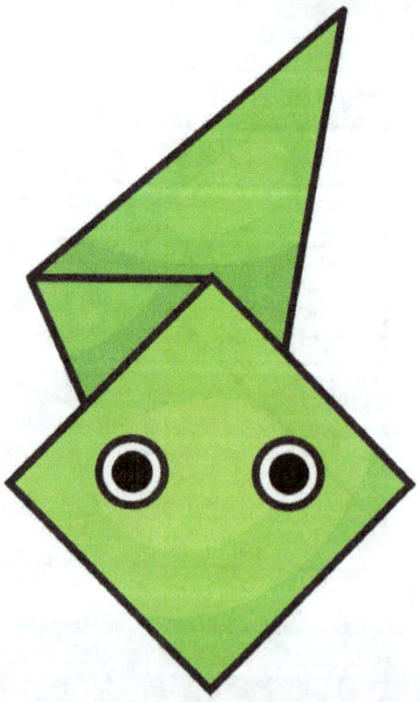

Turtle

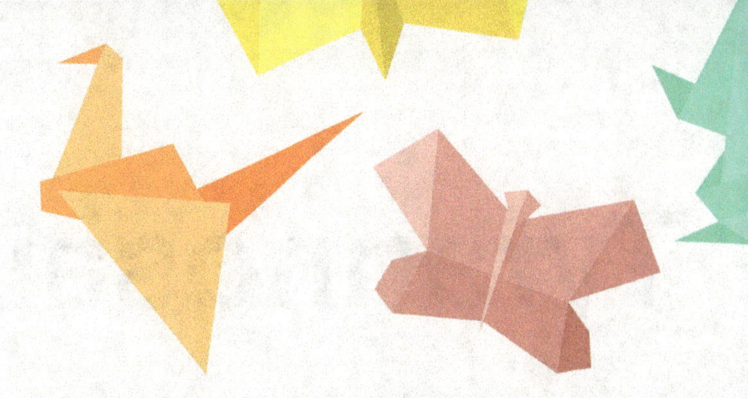

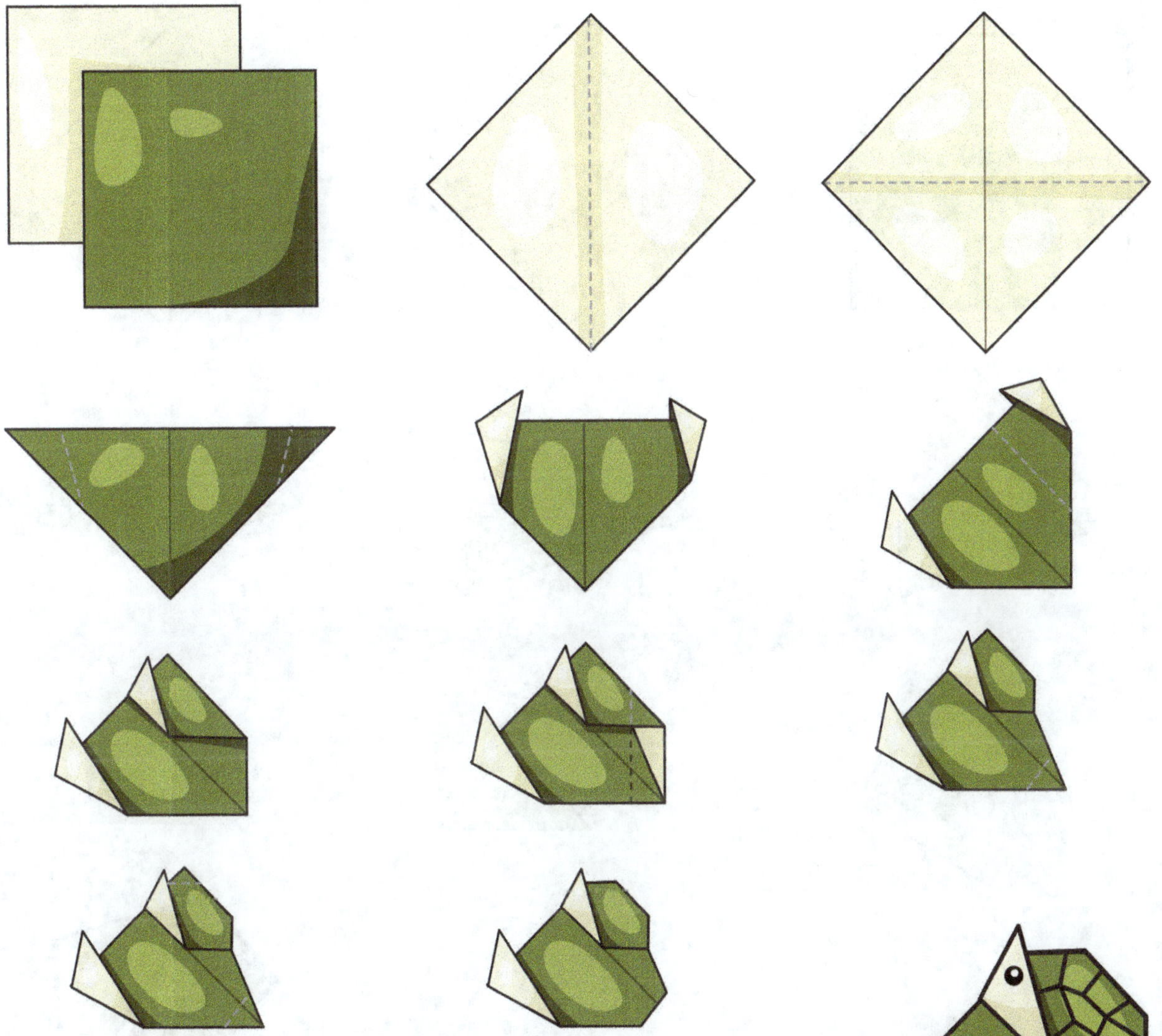

Turtle family

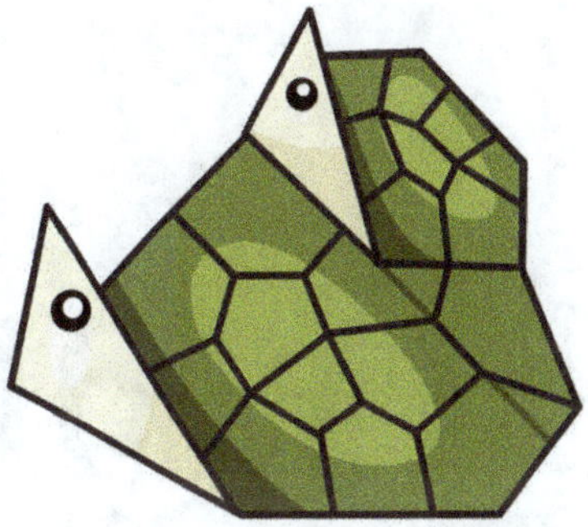

Tyrannosaurus

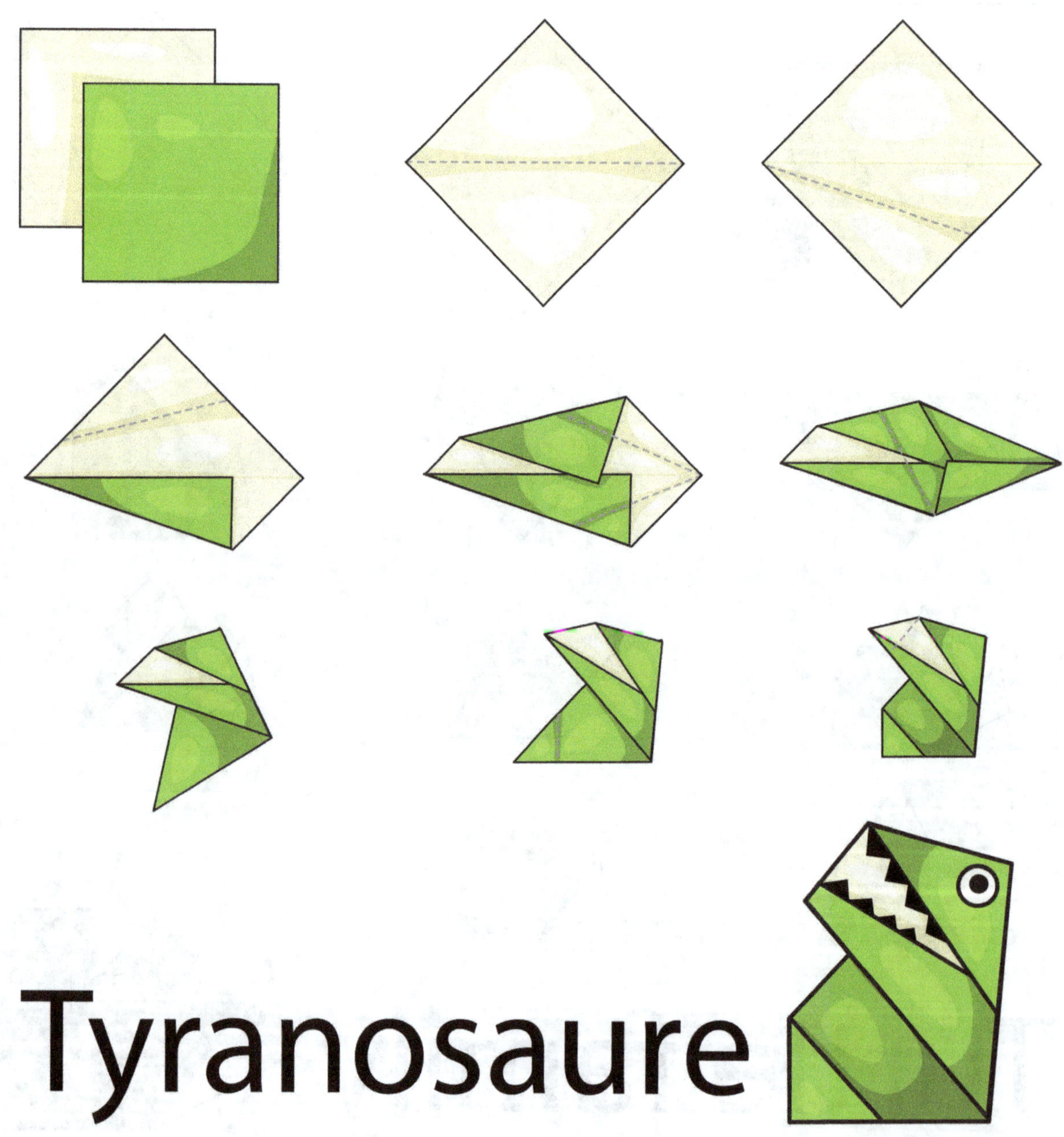

Tyranosaure

Water Melon

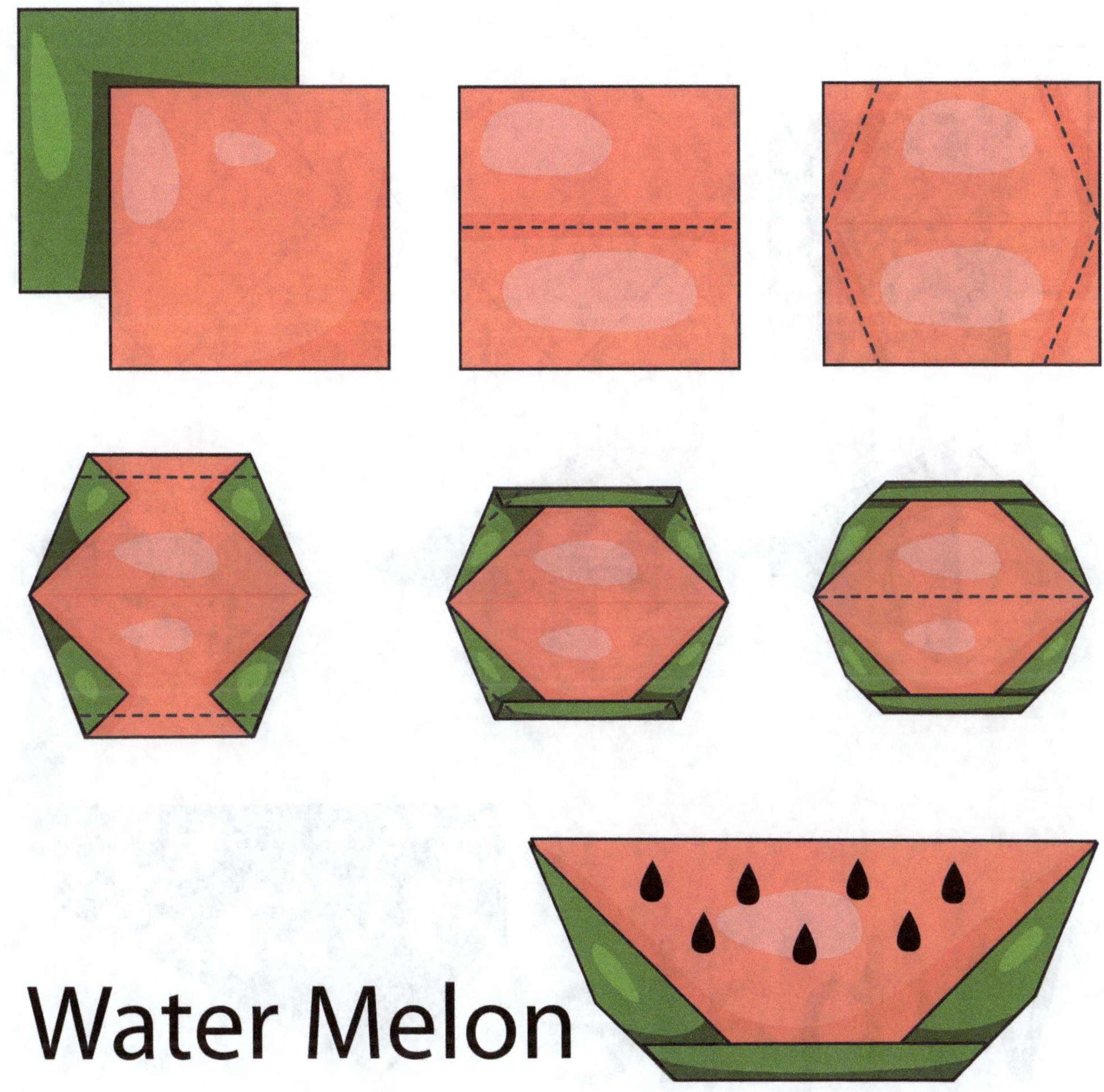

Water Melon

Whale

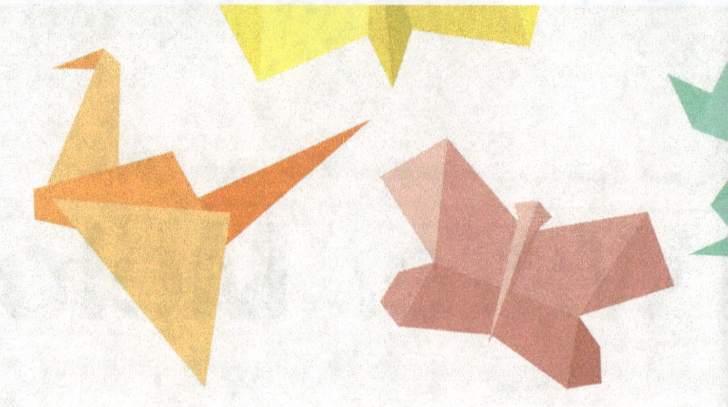

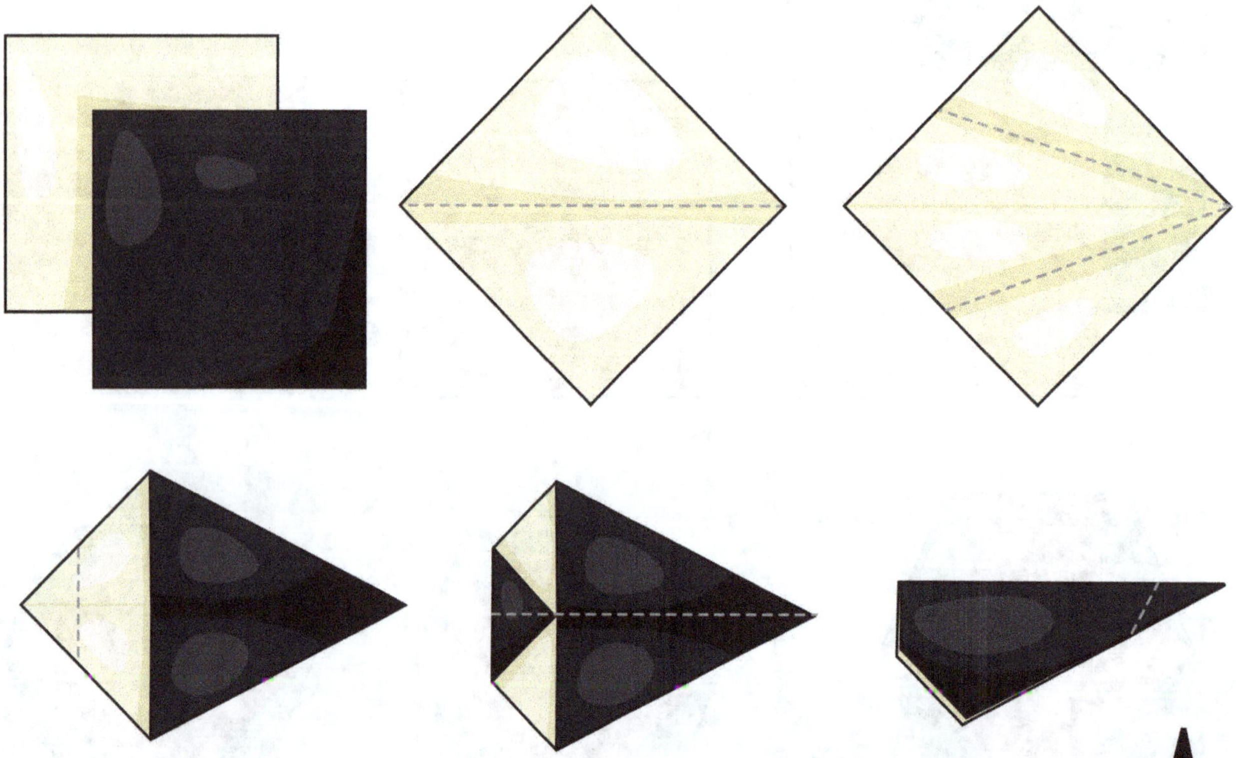

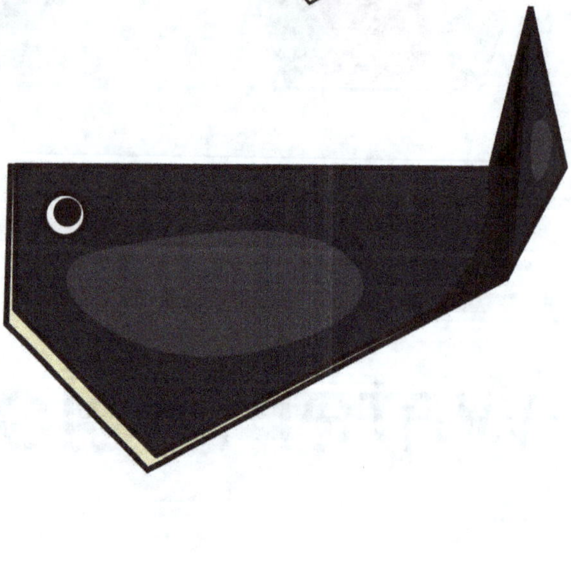

Whale

Whale

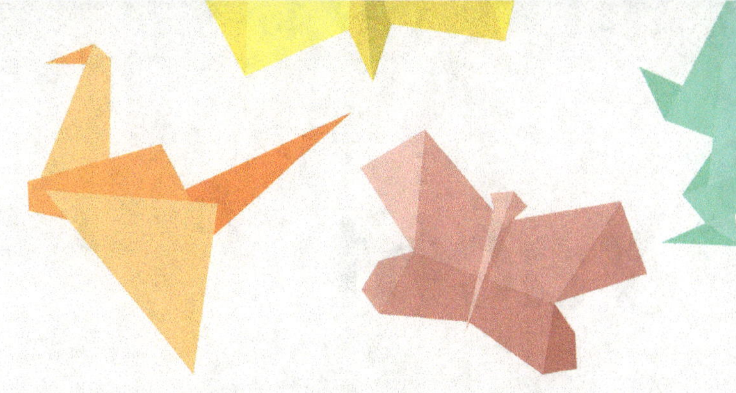

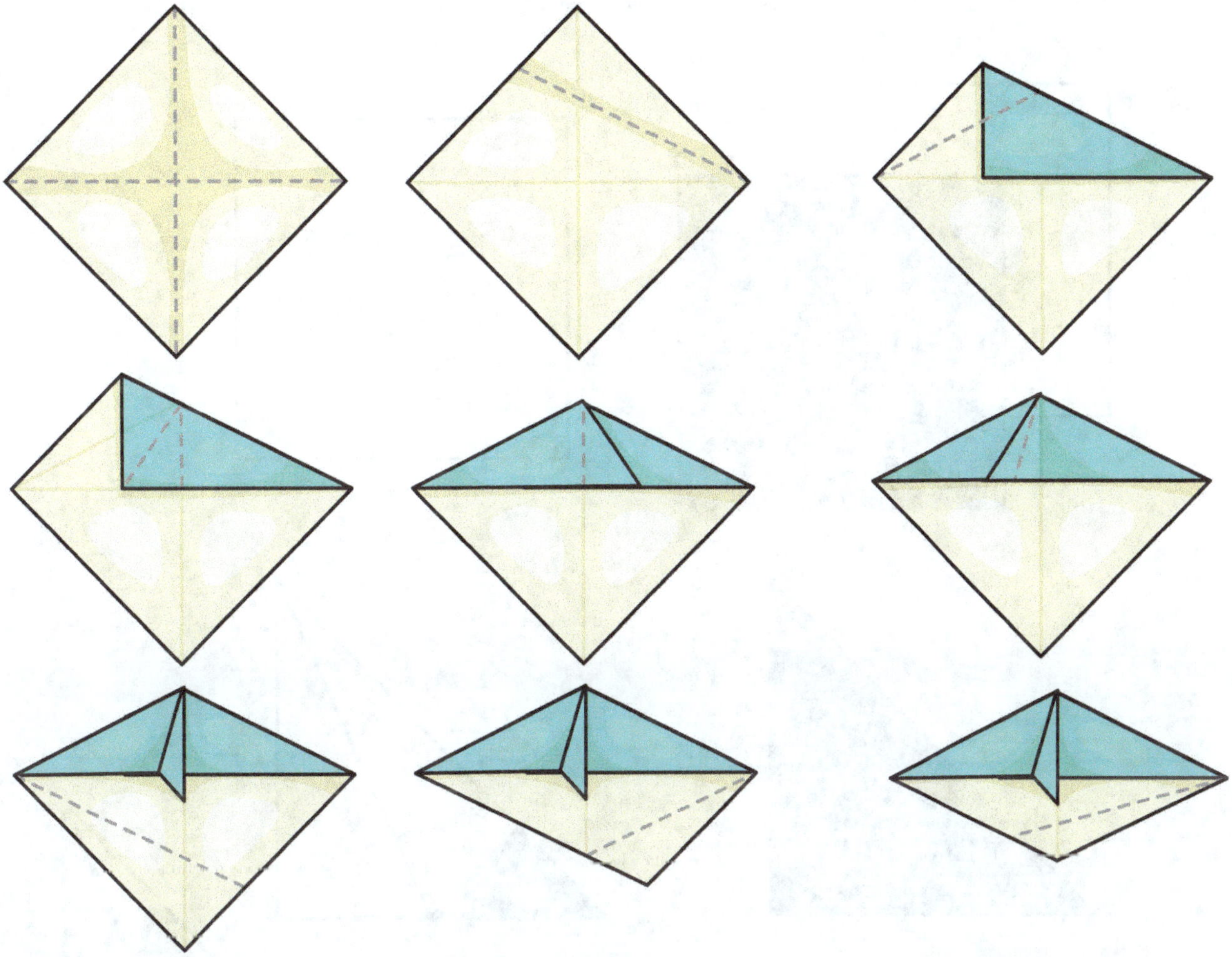

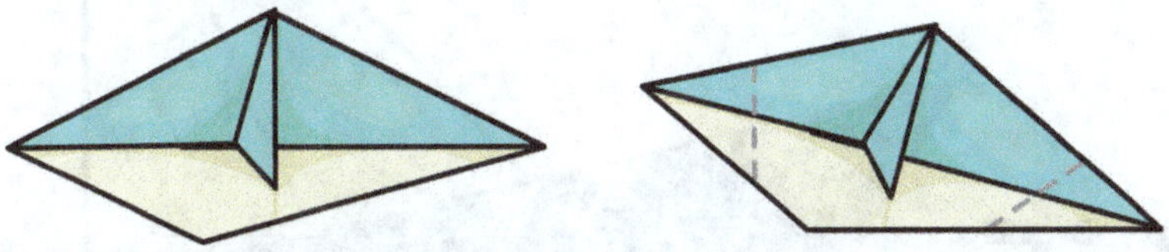

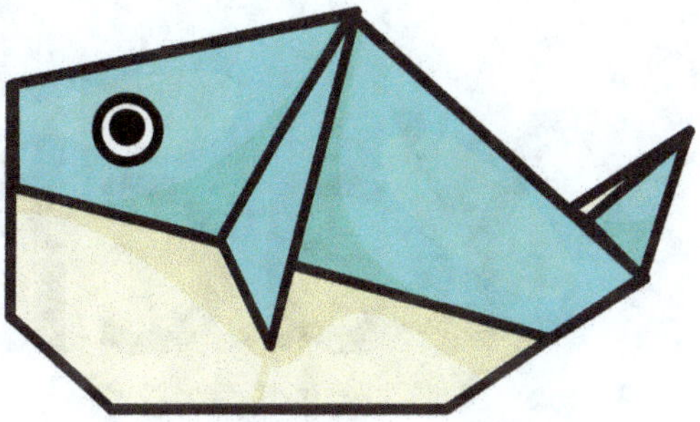

Whale 2

Yacht

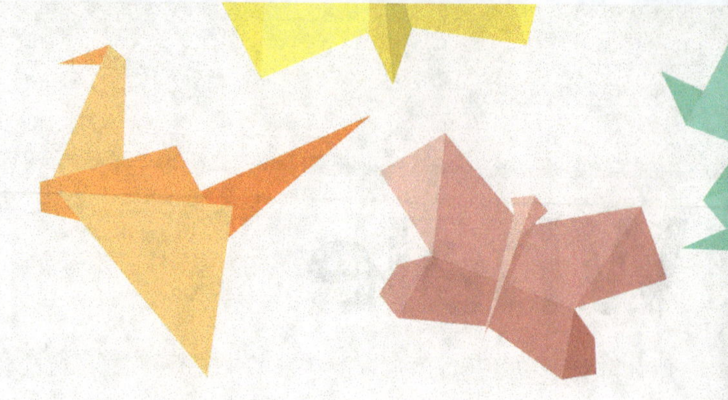

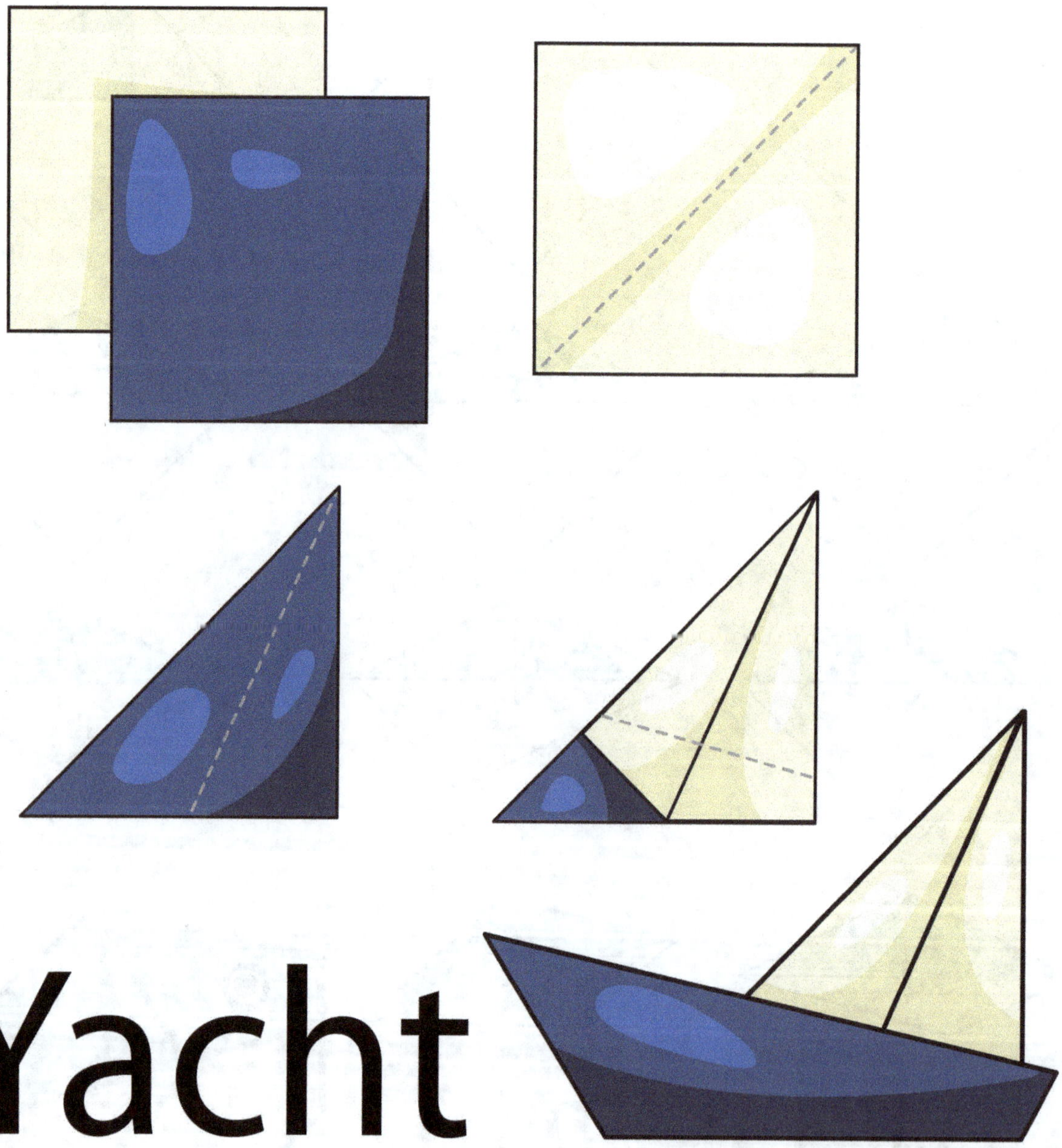

Yacht